THE WORLD CUP
QUIZ BOOK

THE WORLD CUP QUIZ BOOK

Compiled by Adam Pearson

Foreword by Martin Peters MBE

APEX PUBLISHING LTD

First published in 2010, Updated and Reprinted in 2010 by

Apex Publishing Ltd

PO Box 7086, Clacton on Sea, Essex, CO15 5WN, England

www.apexpublishing.co.uk

British Library Cataloguing-in-Publication Data
A catalogue record for this book
is available from the British Library

ISBN HARDBACK: 1-904444-92-X   978-1-904444-92-3

Typeset in 10.5pt Gill Sans MT

Cover Design: Siobhan Smith

Printed in Great Britain by the MPG Books Group, Bodmin and King's Lynn

I would like to dedicate this book to the following...

My friend Stuart Haigh, The Oracle of all football knowledge
who will find this book a doddle.

To everyone at my club Osborne Coburg FC for still keeping the club going.

My friend Ian Coughtrey who has stayed loyal and in touch despite being in Wales.

Darren White who saved me from Morrisons.

My wonderful dog Tigger who passed away while this book was being written.

My new dog Magic who joined the family the day after the book was finished.

My man at Apex Publishing Ltd, Chris Cowlin for his continuing support.

Troy Brown for making this all possible by allowing me to publish his diary.

FOREWORD

I am delighted to write this foreword as the publishers, Apex Publishing Ltd and the compiler Adam Pearson, have agreed to donate £1 from each book sale to the Willow Foundation, a charity set up by Scotland & Arsenal goalkeeper Bob Wilson and his wife Megs in 1999. The Charity enables seriously ill young adults to enjoy the treat of a 'Special Day' with family and friends. For more information on the Willow Foundation please see the back of this book.

I played 67 times for England scoring 20 goals in my international career, and was fortunate to play a part in winning the World Cup in 1966 – an amazing 4-2 win against West Germany. I also played in the 1970 World Cup campaign and have played alongside some fantastic players as well as against superstars like Pele.

When I read through this book I was amazed at all the facts and figures on World Cup history. The questions brought back some great memories from some fantastic matches and players who have played in that fantastic tournament. This book will test your knowledge and see how good your memory is - the 1,000 questions cover everything from players and goal scorers to venues and score-lines.

I hope you enjoy this book as much as I did!

Best wishes
Martin Peters MBE
England (67 Caps, 20 Goals)

INTRODUCTION

My first memories of the World Cup are of a fleeting glimpse of the 1974 World Cup final and my considerable disappointment at the West German victory. I remembered seeing the Olympic Stadium that stuck in my mind from the 1972 Olympic Games. The first World Cup that really sticks in my memory was the 1978 finals in Argentina. All the games were played either late at night or in the early hours of the morning. I was twelve years old and delighted that my grandparents (and legal guardians) allowed me to stay up and watch the games. A game that comes to mind was a tie between France and Argentina. The latter won the game 2-1 but it was a fantastic match. Of course most Brits blindly believed the songs bandied around claiming that Scotland were going to bring the World Cup home but, in the end, Scotland underachieved despite being placed in a 'easy' group. They did, though defeat the eventual losing finalists, Holland. The finals will also be remembered for the ticker tape, confetti that rained down every time Argentina played.

For me the World Cup is a celebration of my game, a pilgrimage that I undertake in front of my television. I would prefer it if England took part in it but, to be honest, I have enjoyed the tournaments without the pressure of watching England games, most of the time. When the Three Lions are partaking, it is wonderful seeing the Flag of St George fluttering away on people's car windows.

I would also like to say how honoured I was that Martin Peters agreed to write the foreword for this book. What more could I ask for than a player from my own country that has not only scored in two World Cup tournaments, but in the final itself in 1966?

Researching this book brought back lots of happy memories and helped old heroes from my distant past to resurface for the super World Cup buff out there. Good luck and enjoy the challenge of the World Cup Quiz Book.

Best wishes

Adam Pearson

ORIGINS

1. What name was given to the original World Cup trophy, first used at the 1930 World Cup finals in Uruguay before it was changed to the Jules Rimet Cup?

2. What was the name of the sculptor who made the World Cup trophy in 1930?

3. What was the name of the man (whose name adorns the UEFA Championship trophy) who vigorously argued that there should be a World football tournament?

4. What was the main reason for starting the World Cup?

5. In 1909 a Tea Tycoon organised an international football competition that is often referred to as the first World Cup, who was he?

6. Which European city hosted the "The First World Cup" in 1909?

7. Which nation won the Olympic football tournaments of 1924 and 1928 and helped to inspire the World Cup competition?

8. Which six nations applied to host the first FIFA World Cup?

9. In which city did Jules Rimet hand over the brand new World Cup trophy to Dr Raul Jude of the Uruguayan FA in 1930?

10. What surviving Greek masterpiece was the original World Cup trophy based upon?

URUGUAY 1930

11. Which two nations (one South American one European) contested the opening game of the 1930 World Cup finals?

12. What was the name of the stadium that staged the opening game of the 1930 World Cup finals?

13. What makes Montevideo unique in World Cup history apart from being the first city to stage a World Cup match?

14. Which nation beat both Paraguay and Belgium in Group 4 to progress to the semi finals of the 1930 World Cup?

15. Which nation beat both Romania and Peru in Group 3 to progress to the semi finals of the 1930 World Cup?

16. Which nation beat both Brazil and Bolivia in Group 2 to progress to the semi finals of the 1930 World Cup?

17. Which nation beat Chile, France and Mexico in Group 1 to progress to the semi finals of the 1930 World Cup?

18. Both 1930 World Cup semi finals were seven goal thrillers and finished with identical score lines. What was that score line?

19. What was the name of the stadium that was completed half way through the 1930 World Cup finals that staged the very first World Cup final?

20. Who scored the first ever goal in a World Cup final when Uruguay beat Argentina 4-2 in 1930?

JULES RIMET

21. What year did Jules Rimet become President of FIFA?

22. Where was Jules Rimet born?

23. What profession was Jules Rimet practising at the turn of the 1900s?

24. What decoration did Jules Rimet earn during the First World War?

25. What year was Jules Rimet replaced as President of FIFA?

26. How tall in inches was the Jules Rimet trophy?

27. What year was Jules Rimet nominated for a Nobel prize?

28. In what Swiss city did Jules Rimet open the 1954 World Cup tournament?

29. In what year was the Jules Rimet trophy stolen for the second time, never to be seen again?

30. Jules Rimet died two days after his 83rd birthday in what year?

ITALY 1934

31. Who was Italy's Fascist dictator at the time of the 1934 World Cup?

32. What was the name of Italy's coach for the 1934 World Cup?

33. In what Rome stadium was the 1934 World Cup Final staged?

34. Which nation did Italy beat in the opening game of the 1934 World Cup finals?

35. How many nations competed in the 1934 World Cup?

36. Brazil was one of eight nations to only play one match in the 1934 World Cup finals. Why was that?

37. In which Milan stadium did Italy knock Austria out of the 1934 World Cup semi-final?

38. The first African nation to take part in a World Cup did so in 1934, which country was that?

39. Most of South America boycotted the 1934 World Cup. Only Brazil and which other nation took part?

40. Which Czech player scored five goals during the 1934 World Cup?

FRANCE 1938

41.   Why did Spain pull out of the 1938 World Cup before the qualification rounds?

42.   When Austria had to pull out of the 1938 World Cup because of being annexed by Germany, which country did FIFA unsuccessfully offer Austria's place in the finals?

43.   How many nations competed in the 1938 World Cup finals?

44.   In which stadium did Switzerland and Germany kick off the last pre war World Cup finals tournament?

45.   Which nation played it's one and only match in a World Cup finals tournament when it lost 6-0 to Hungary on June 5th 1938?

46.   Which two nations represented the Americas during the 1938 World Cup finals?

47.   What stadium staged the 1938 World Cup final between Italy and Hungary?

48.   What was the final score of the 1938 World Cup final between Italy and Hungary?

49.   By what other name was the World Cup competition known in 1938?

50.   Which nations played out the third-place play-off in 1938?

BRAZIL 1950

51. What was the 'Official' capacity of the Maracanã Stadium in Rio?

52. What was the attendance of the 1950 World Cup final?

53. What was the final score of England's first ever match in a World Cup finals tournament against Chile in 1950?

54. Which nation won England's pool (group) in the 1950 World Cup finals?

55. Which nation finished bottom of the Final Pool table in the 1950 World Cup?

56. What was the name of the player who scored the most goals in the 1950 World Cup finals?

57. How many nations competed in the 1950 World Cup finals?

58. Who scored USA's historic winning goal against England in the 1950 World Cup?

59. Who scored Brazil's goal in the 1950 World Cup final?

60. What was the final score of the 1950 World Cup final?

SWITZERLAND 1954

61.   What nation returned to the World Cup finals of 1954 after its ban was lifted in 1950?

62.   Which nation beat Scotland 7-0 in the 1954 World Cup finals?

63.   Which Hungarian scored the opening goal of the 1954 World Cup final against West Germany?

64.   Which nation finished fourth in the 1954 World Cup?

65.   Which nation represented Asia in the 1954 World Cup?

66.   A Hungarian striker was the top goal scorer in the 1954 World Cup, how many goals did he score?

67.   1954 World Cup finalists had previously met in the group stage of the tournament with Hungary beating the future Champions, West Germany in a match that saw eleven goals. What was the final score of that encounter?

68.   What was the name of the stadium that hosted the 1954 World Cup final?

69.   Who scored the winning goal of the 1954 World Cup final?

70.   What was the name of the West German captain in the 1954 World Cup finals?

FERENC PUSKÁS

71.   What year was Ferenc Puskás born?

72.   How many International caps did Ferenc Puskás win? A: 87, B: 97, C: 107, D: 117.

73.   Which non-Hungarian club did Ferenc Puskás play for?

74.   In what Hungarian city was Ferenc Puskás born?

75.   For which country did Ferenc Puskás play for in the 1962 World Cup finals?

76.   How many goals did Ferenc Puskás score for Hungary in his career? A: 53, B: 63, C: 73, D: 83.

77.   What was the name of the Hungarian club that Ferenc Puskás played for?

78.   By what nickname was Ferenc Puskás known?

79.   In what year did Ferenc Puskás defect to the West?

80.   In what year did Ferenc Puskás retire as a player?

SWEDEN 1958

81. What was the name of the French player who was top goal scorer in the 1958 World Cup finals?

82. How many goals did Brazilian legend Pelé score in the 1958 World Cup finals?

83. What was the final score of the 1958 World Cup final?

84. England played out two 2-2 draws in Pool 4 of the 1958 World Cup finals, against which nations?

85. What was the name of the Brazilian captain who lifted the World Cup in 1958?

86. Which Home Nation was the only British side to record a victory in the 1958 World Cup?

87. Which nation knocked Wales out of the 1958 World Cup quarter-final?

88. In which Swedish city was the 1958 World Cup final played?

89. What was the name of the Northern Ireland player who scored five goals in of his nation's six the 1958 World Cup finals?

90. Which nation finished third in the 1958 World Cup?

RAYMOND KOPA

91.   For what nation did Raymond Kopa play?

92.   With which club did Raymond Kopa win two league titles in his native country?

93.   In what year did Raymond Kopa win the European Player of the Year Award?

94.   Which club did Raymond Kopa play for outside France?

95.   Which honour makes Raymond Kopa unique in World Cup history?

96.   What longer family name was Raymond Kopa's surname shortened from?

97.   Which town was Raymond Kopa born?

98.   Which footballing legend named Raymond Kopa in his list of 125 top living footballers in March 2004?

99.   In which year did Raymond Kopa play his last game for France?

100.   On how many occasions did Raymond Kopa win the European Champions Cup?

JUST FONTAINE

101. What World Cup record did Just Fontaine still hold in 2008?

102. Where was Just Fontaine born?

103. At which club did Just Fontaine begin his professional playing career?

104. How many goals did Just Fontaine score in his 21 games for France?

105. Which two national teams has Just Fontaine managed?

106. Which French club did Just Fontaine manage between 1973 and 1976?

107. How old was Just Fontaine when he was forced to retire as a player after breaking his leg?

108. At which club did Just Fontaine begin his career as an amateur?

109. Which club did Just Fontaine join in 1956?

110. What year was Just Fontaine born?

PELÉ (PART 1)

111.   What is Pelé's full name?

112.   Where in Brazil was Pelé born?

113.   What year did Pelé win his only individual honour, that of
        South American Player of the Year?

114.   Which Brazilian club did Pelé play for?

115.   In how many World Cup finals tournaments did Pelé play?

116.   How many first class goals did Pelé score during his career?

117.   How many goals did Pelé score in all of his appearances in
        World Cup finals tournaments?

118.   Against which country did Pelé score his first goal in the
        World Cup finals of 1958?

119.   Against which country did Pelé score a hat trick in the 1958
        World Cup finals tournament?

120.   What political position did Pelé take up after he had retired
        from football?

CHILE 1962

121. Which South American nation did England beat 3-1 in the group stage of the 1962 World Cup finals?

122. Which nation gained a creditable 0-0 draw in the group stage against reigning World Champions Brazil at the 1962 World Cup finals?

123. Who was the Hungarian who scored a hat trick in a 6-1 win in the group stage of the 1962 World Cup against Bulgaria?

124. How many goals did Pelé score in the 1962 World Cup?

125. Which Brazilian player scored four goals in total in the Quarter-Finals and Semi-Finals of the 1962 World Cup?

126. Because six players scored four goals each as top scorers in the 1962 World Cup they drew lots to decide who won the Top Scorer Prize, whose name came out of the draw?

127. What was the name of the English referee that sent off Italy's Mario David and Georgio Ferrini against Chile in Group B in the 1962 World Cup finals?

128. What nickname did Brazil's Amarildo earn in the 1962 World Cup finals?

129. Which nation finished third in the 1962 World Cup?

130. Which nation knocked West Germany out of the 1962 World Cup Quarter-Finals?

GARRINCHA

131.   What was Garrincha's real name?

132.   What club did Garrincha make 581 appearances for between 1953 and 1965?

133.   In Brazil the popular Garrincha was known as Alegria do Povo what does that translate to?

134.   What was the name of the Samba singer that Garrincha met and fell in love with during the 1962 World Cup?

135.   What year did Garrincha win his first cap for Brazil?

136.   How many caps did Garrincha win for Brazil?

137.   How many children in Garrincha 'known' to have fathered?

138.   In what year did Garrincha play his last international match for Brazil?

139.   What year did Garrincha's professional playing career end?

140.   How old was Garrincha when he died of Cirrhosis of the Liver in 1983?

ENGLAND 1966

141. Which Englishman was President of FIFA in 1966?

142. What was the name of the mascot for the 1966 World Cup?

143. In which city did Brazil play their World Cup finals games of 1966?

144. Which team qualified for the World Cup quarter-finals along with England in group 1 in the 1966 World Cup finals?

145. What stadium hosted just one game in Group 1 of the 1966 World Cup finals?

146. Who was top goal scorer in the 1966 World Cup finals?

147. Which nation qualified from Group 4 along with the Soviet Union in the 1966 World Cup finals?

148. Who was runner-up for the Golden Boot in the 1966 World Cup?

149. Who was manager of West Germany in the 1966 World Cup?

150. Which stadium, apart from Wembley, hosted a World Cup semi-final in 1966?

JACK CHARLTON

151. For how many years did Jack Charlton play first team football at Leeds United?

152. What was the first club that Jack Charlton was asked to manage?

153. Jack Charlton's uncle played for Newcastle United and England, who was he?

154. What profession did Jack Charlton quit before being taken on by Leeds United?

155. In what year did Jack Charlton play his last game for England?

156. In what year did Jack Charlton win the Footballer of the Year award?

157. Who did Jack Charlton replace as manager of the Republic of Ireland?

158. In what year was Jack Charlton born?

159. In what year did Jack Charlton make his debut for England?

160. How many times did Jack Charlton win a European Fairs Cup medal?

EUSÉBIO

161. What was Eusébio's full name?

162. In what country was Eusébio born?

163. What club did Eusébio play for between 1960 and 1975?

164. By what nickname was Eusébio known?

165. In what year did Eusébio win the European Footballer of the Year award?

166. In what year did Eusébio win the European Champions Cup against Real Madrid?

167. In what year did Eusébio play his last game for Portugal?

168. How many World Cup Finals tournaments did Eusébio play in?

169. Eusébio is Portugal's all time top goal scorer, how many goals did he score for his national side? A: 31, B: 41, C: 51, D:61.

170. In what year was Eusébio born?

SIR ALF RAMSAY

171.   Alf Ramsay was a World Cup finals player in which year?

172.   Where was Alf Ramsay born?

173.   What year did Sir Alf Ramsay pass away?

174.   At which club was Alf Ramsay playing when he won his first England cap?

175.   At which club was Alf Ramsay playing when he won most of his England caps?

176.   Which club did Alf Ramsay managing when he became England manager?

177.   Which club did Alf Ramsay manage in 1977-78?

178.   In what year was Sir Alf Ramsay sacked as manager of England?

179.   Which continental club was Sir Alf Ramsay appointed as technical advisor in 1979?

180.   What position did Alf Ramsay play for club and country?

SIR BOBBY CHARLTON

181.   Which club did Bobby Charlton manage in 1973-74?

182.   What year was Bobby Charlton born?

183.   What Irish club did Bobby Charlton play for in 1975?

184.   How many England caps did Bobby Chalrton win?

185.   What year did Bobby Charlton become a director of Manchester United FC?

186.   How many World Cup finals squads was Bobby Charlton selected for?

187.   Against which nation did Bobby Charlton win his last England cap while playing in the 1970 World Cup?

188.   Which England player emerged as a child talent after winning a competition in one of Bobby Charlton's soccer schools?

189.   What is the name of Bobby Charlton's weather forecaster daughter who appeared on BBCTV?

190.   In what year was Bobby Charlton knighted?

SIR GEOFF HURST

191. What is Geoff Hurst's middle name?

192. In what year did Geoff Hurst join West Ham United?

193. For which county did Geoff Hurst play one first class cricket match for in 1962?

194. Which club did Geoff Hurst join when he left West Ham in 1972?

195. Geoff Hurst scored just one goal for England in the 1970 World Cup finals, against which nation?

196. How many caps did Geoff Hurst win with England? A: 49, B: 59, C: 69, D: 79.

197. With which club did Geoff Hurst end his playing career in England?

198. Which club did Geoff Hurst manage between 1979 and 1981?

199. In which county was Geoff Hurst born?

200. What was the name of the German goalkeeper who conceded Geoff Hurst's historic hat-trick in the 1966 World Cup final?

FRANZ BECKENBAUER

201.   In what year was Franz Beckenbauer born?

202.   Franz Beckenbauer played for two German clubs, Bayern Munich and who else?

203.   How many caps did Franz Beckenbauer win for West Germany? A: 73, B: 83, C: 93, D: 103.

204.   In what year did Franz Beckenbauer play his last international match?

205.   What USA club did Franz Beckenbauer play for in the 70s and 80s?

206.   Which French club did Franz Beckenbauer manage between 1990 and 1991?

207.   How many World Cup finals tournaments was Franz Beckenbauer involved in as a player and a manager?

208.   What was Franz Beckenbauer's nickname?

209.   How many goals in total did Franz Beckenbauer score in all of his appearances in World Cup finals tournaments?

210.   Franz Beckenbauer won three consecutive European Champions cups with Bayern Munich, what years did he achieve that?

MEXICO 1970

211.   Mexico opened the 1970 World Cup tournament with a 0-0 draw against whom?

212.   England began their defence of the World Cup in 1970 with a 1-0 win against which nation?

213.   Which West German player scored hat tricks in two consecutive games in the 1970 World Cup finals?

214.   Which nation was the only side to fail to score against Brazil during the 1970 World Cup finals?

215.   Which nation qualified as winners of Group Two in the 1970 World Cup despite only having scored one goal in the three games?

216.   Cubillas came third in the top scorers chart of the 1970 World Cup finals, what country did he play for?

217.   Which nations played in the Third Place play off in the 1970 World Cup finals?

218.   Which nation's final stats for the 1970 World Cup finals was played: 3, lost: 3, goals for: 0, goals against: 9?

219.   Who did Italy beat 4-1 in the World Cup quarter final of 1970?

220.   Which Brazilian star scored in every one of his country's games in the 1970 World Cup finals?

JAIRZINHO

221. What was Jairzinho's birth name?

222. Jairzinho played alongside his childhood hero in the 1966 Word Cup, who was that?

223. Jairzinho made his debut for Brazil in 1964, what year did he win his last cap?

224. What French club did Jairzinho join in 1974?

225. Jairzinho scored Brazil's first goal of the 1974 World Cup finals, against whom?

226. What year was Jairzinho born?

227. How many goals did Jairzinho score for Brazil in his career? A: 23, B: 33, C: 43, D: 53.

228. Who was the 14 year old that Jairzinho spotted while coaching São Cristóvão who went on to win the World Cup with Brazil?

229. Against which nation did Jairzinho score his last World Cup goal for Brazil?

230. Which of Brazil's four goals in the 1970 World Cup Final against Italy did Jairzinho score? A: 1st, B: 2nd, C: 3rd, D: 4th.

BOBBY MOORE

231. One of Bobby Moore's middle names is also the name of a London football club, what is it?

232. What year did Bobby Moore win the European Cup Winners Cup with West Ham?

233. Which English league club did Bobby Moore once manage?

234. In what country was Bobby Moore once accused of stealing a bracelet from a jeweller?

235. What year did Bobby Moore make his debut for West Ham United?

236. What year did Bobby Moore win the Footballer of the Year award?

237. Who did Bobby Moore overtake when he became the West Ham player to have played the most games for the club on February 17th 1973?

238. How much did Fulham pay West Ham when they signed Bobby Moore in 1974? A: Free Transfer, B: £2,500, C: £25,000, D: £250,000.

239. In what year did Bobby Moore play his last game for Fulham?

240. What year did Bobby Moore pass away?

CARLOS ALBERTO

241.   Which national team did Carlos Alberto coach?

242.   What was Carlos Alberto's full name?

243.   What year was Carlos Alberto born?

244.   What USA team did Carlos Alberto play for between 1977 and 1980?

245.   What year did Carlos Alberto make his international debut for Brazil?

246.   For which Brazilian club did Carlos Alberto play between 1966 and 1974?

247.   How many goals did Carlos Alberto score for Brazil? A: 2, B: 4, C: 6, D: 8.

248.   In what year did Carlos Alberto play his last game for Brazil?

249.   How many caps did Carlos Alberto win playing for Brazil? A: 43, B: 53, C: 63, D: 73.

250.   What year did Carlos Alberto retire as a player?

PELÉ (PART 2)

251. Who did Pelé regard as the best defender he ever played against?

252. What year was Pelé born?

253. Which English club was Pelé linked to as their chief South American scout?

254. How many goals did Pelé score for Brazil in his career? A: 47, B: 57, C: 67, D: 77.

255. What year did Pelé make his international debut?

256. Pelé is one of only two players to have scored in four different World Cup tournaments, who is the other?

257. Pelé starred alongside his friend Bobby Moore in which 1981 wartime film?

258. In which British comedy film did Pelé make a cameo appearance in 2001?

259. In what year was Pelé awarded the KBE, an honorary knighthood by Great Britain?

260. What English Premiership football club did Pelé scout for in 2002?

WEST GERMANY 1974

261.   Who were the 'whipping boys' of the 1974 World Cup finals, conceding 14 goals and scoring none?

262.   Who scored Scotland's first goal in the 1974 World Cup Finals?

263.   Who scored West Germany's first goal in the 1974 World Cup finals?

264.   West Germany qualified for the Semi-final group of the 1974 World Cup as runners-up of Group A, who won the group?

265.   Which team was beaten 3-1 by Italy, 7-0 by Poland and 4-1 by Argentina in the 1974 World Cup finals group D?

266.   Who was top goal scorer in the 1974 World Cup Finals with 7 goals?

267.   What was the name of the English referee who officiated the 1974 World Cup final?

268.   Who was the first player to be sent off by being shown a red card in a World Cup finals tournament in 1974?

269.   In which stadium was the 1974 World Cup final played?

270.   What was the only nation to end the 1974 World Cup with an unbeaten record?

JOHAN CRUYFF

271.   What is Johan Cryuff's full name?

272.   What year was Johan Cryuff born?

273.   Which club did Johan Cryuff join when he left Ajax
        Amsterdam in 1973?

274.   What USA club did Johan Cryuff join in 1979?

275.   In what year did Johan Cryuff make his debut for Ajax
        Amsterdam?

276.   What year did Johan Cryuff win his first cap with Holland?

277.   With which club did Johan Cryuff end his playing career in
        1984?

278.   How many times did Johan Cryuff win the European
        Champions Cup as a player and a coach?

279.   How many times did Johan Cryuff win domestic league titles
        while playing or coaching European clubs?

280.   When Johan Cryuff won the European Footballer of the Year
        in 1971, who did he succeed in the award?

GERD MÜLLER

281.   Which club did Gerd Müller play for between 1964 and 1979?

282.   How many goals did Gerd Müller score for West Germany in 62 appearances? A: 38, B: 48, C: 58, D: 68.

283.   How many goals did Gerd Müller score for his club in West Germany? A: 203, B: 303, C: 403, D: 503.

284.   What honour, other than the 1974 World Cup, did Gerd Müller win with West Germany?

285.   What year did Gerd Müller win the World Greatest All-time goal scorer award?

286.   How many times did Gerd Müller win the European Champions Cup?

287.   What USA club did Gerd Müller play for at the end of his career?

288.   How many goals did Gerd Müller score in the 1970 and 1974 World Cup finals combined?

289.   What year did Gerd Müller make his debut for West Germany?

290.   By what nickname was Gerd Müller known?

ARGENTINA 1978

291. Who scored Italy's first goal of the 1978 World Cup finals?

292. Who was the referee that represented Wales at the 1978 World Cup finals?

293. What was the only nation to beat Argentina at the 1978 World Cup finals?

294. Who was the top goal scorer in the 1978 World Cup finals after scoring six goals?

295. Which nation only scored one goal in the 1978 World Cup finals tournament?

296. What significance in World Cup history does Rob Resenbrink's goal for Holland against Scotland have?

297. Who was the Scottish international who was expelled from the 1978 World Cup finals after had been found to have taken a banned stimulant during a the game against Peru?

298. An African nation won a World Cup finals match for the first time in 1978, which one?

299. What, now established, football event was first introduced for the 1978 World Cup finals but was never put into practise?

300. Who scored Argentina's opening goal of the 1978 World Cup finals tournament against Hungary in Group 1?

MARIO KEMPES

301.   In what year was Mario Kempes born?

302.   Which Spanish club did Mario Kempes have two spells with between 1977-1981 and 1982-1984?

303.   Who was Mario Kempes's manager with Argentina during the 1978 World Cup?

304.   What year did Mario Kempes make his international debut?

305.   In how many World Cup finals tournaments did Mario Kempes play?

306.   By what nickname was Mario Kempes known?

307.   At which Argentinian club ad Mario Kempes begin his career?

308.   Against which nation did Mario Kempes score his last ever goal in World Cup finals?

309.   How many goals did Mario Kempes score in all of the World Cup finals tournaments he played in?

310.   What was Mario Kempes's middle name? A: Philipo, B: Armondo, C: Alberto, D: Roberto.

ARCHIE GEMMILL

311.   At which club did Archie Gemmill begin his professional career?

312.   What was the first English club to employ Archie Gemmill's services?

313.   What number shirt was Archie Gemmill wearing when he scored his wonder goal against Holland in the 1978 World Cup finals?

314.   Which club did Archie Gemmill join when he left Nottingham Forest in 1979?

315.   What USA club did Archie Gemmill play for in 1982?

316.   When Archie Gemmill scored his wonder goal against Holland in the 1978 World Cup finals. Who did a play a one-two with before he went on to score?

317.   What is the name of Archie Gemmill's Scottish international son?

318.   With which club did Archie Gemmill end his playing career in 1984?

319.   How many Scotland caps did Archie Gemmill win? A: 33, B: 43, C: 53, D: 63.

320.   In what year was Archie Gemmill born?

OSVALDO ARDILES

321. From what club did Tottenham Hotspur sign Osvaldo Ardiles in 1978?

322. In what year did Osvaldo Ardiles make his debut for Argentina?

323. What was the first club that Osvaldo Ardiles managed?

324. Which French club did Osvaldo Ardiles join on loan in 1982-83?

325. What was reason that Osvaldo Ardiles left Tottenham Hotspur on loan in 1982-83?

326. What was Osvaldo Ardiles's squad number in the 1982 World Cup finals?

327. What English club did Osvaldo Ardiles join in 1987?

328. What was Osvaldo Ardiles's nickname in his native Argentina?

329. What club did Osvaldo Ardiles leave when he became manager of Tottenham Hotspur?

330. What is the only Argentinian club to employ Osvaldo Ardiles as their manager?

SPAIN 1982

331.   Who scored the first goal of the 1982 World Cup finals?

332.   Who scored twice in Scotland's 5-2 victory against New Zealand in the 1982 World Cup finals?

333.   Who scored Northern Ireland's winning goal against hosts Spain in Group 5 in the 1982 World Cup finals?

334.   Who scored on Brazil's first and last match of the 1982 World Cup finals tournament?

335.   Who was top goal scorer in the 1982 World Cup finals?

336.   Which team qualified for the second round of the 1982 World Cup finals after having drawn all three of their games in Group 1?

337.   Which nation did Italy beat in the Semi-Final of the 1982 World Cup finals?

338.   What stadium hosted the 1982 World Cup final?

339.   Who scored West Germany's consolation goal in the 1982 World Cup final?

340.   Who was second top goal scorer in the 1982 World Cup finals tournament?

PAOLO ROSSI

341. What club was Paolo Rossi playing for when he made his international debut for Italy?

342. What year did Paolo Rossi make his international debut?

343. Who succeeded Paulo Rossi as European Footballer of the Year?

344. Who succeeded Paulo Rossi as World Player of the Year?

345. Which club did Paulo Rossi join when he left Juventus in 1985?

346. How many international goals did Paulo Rossi score in his 48 appearances for his county? A: 10, B: 15, C: 20, D: 25.

347. Why was Paulo Rossi banned from playing for two years in 1980?

348. How many goals did Paulo Rossi score during the 1978 World Cup finals in Argentina?

349. Who was the Italian coach that selected Paolo Rossi for the 1978 Italian World Cup squad?

350. In what year did Paolo Rossi win his last Italian cap?

BRYAN ROBSON

351. In what year did Bryan Robson make his league debut for West Bromwich Albion?

352. Which league club did Bryan Robson manage in 2003-4?

353. In what year did Bryan Robson join Manchester United?

354. Against which nation did Bryan Robson score what was then, the fastest goal in World Cup history in the 1982 finals?

355. Which player broke Bryan Robson's record of the fastest goal in World Cup history when he scored after ten seconds 2002 finals?

356. In how many World Cup finals tournaments did Bryan Robson play?

357. Who did Bryan Robson replace as manager of Middlesborough in 1994?

358. How much did Manchester United pay West Bromwich Albion when they signed Bryan Robson?

359. What was Bryan Robson's nickname?

360. Which trophy did Bryan Robson win with Manchester United in 1991?

GIUSEPPE BERGOMI

361. In what year was Giuseppe Bergomi born?

362. What was the first World Cup finals tournament that Giuseppe Bergomi played in?

363. What was the only club that Giuseppe Bergomi played for?

364. In how many World Cup finals tournaments did Giuseppe Bergomi play?

365. How many caps did Giuseppe Bergomi win with Italy? A: 71, B: 81, C: 91, D: 101.

366. In what year did Giuseppe Bergomi retire from football?

367. What was Giuseppe Bergomi's nickname?

368. Against which nation did Giuseppe Bergomi make his international debut?

369. Giuseppe Bergomi was involved in the fastet substitution in World Cup history, who did he replace in Italy's game against Austria?

370. How many times did Giuseppe Bergomi win the UEFA Cup?

MICHEL PLATINI

371.   What is Michel Platini's full name?

372.   Name one of the French clubs that Michel Platini played for.

373.   In what year did Michel Platini make his debut for France?

374.   True or false - Michel Platini played in the 1976 Olympic Games.

375.   In how many World Cup finals tournaments did Michel Platini play?

376.   Michel Platini captained France to victory in the 1984 against which nation?

377.   In what year was Michel Platini elected as President of UEFA?

378.   How many times did Michel Platini win the European Footballer of the Year award?

379.   Who succeeded Michel Platini as the World Footballer of the Year after he had won the award in consecutive years?

380.   Who did Michel Platini replace as President of UEFA?

DINO ZOFF

381. What year was Dino Zoff born?

382. What World Cup record does Dino Zoff hold?

383. How many caps did Dino Zoff win with Italy? A: 82, B: 92, C: 102, D: 112.

384. Which Italian club has Dino Zoff managed twice?

385. In what year did Dino Zoff make his International debut for Italy?

386. At which club did Dino Zoff begin his professional career?

387. In what year did Dino Zoff become manager of Italy?

388. Dino Zoff held the record for the most appearances in Italian Serie A for 20 years. Who broke his record in 2005-6?

389. In what year did Dino Zoff win a European Championship winners medal with Italy?

390. Who did Dino Zoff replace as manager of Italy?

MEXICO 1986

391.   What nation had originally been chosen to host the 1986 World Cup but couldn't afford it and pulled out?

392.   What was the name of the World Cup mascot for 1986?

393.   What was the Mexican stadium with the largest capacity in the 1986 World Cup finals?

394.   What was the name of the referee who represented England in the 1986 World Cup finals?

395.   Who was the top scorer for the 1986 World Cup finals?

396.   Who scored the first goal of the 1986 World Cup finals for Italy?

397.   Which nation went home from the 1986 without scoring a goal?

398.   Which nation won group F (England's group) in the 1986 World Cup final?

399.   Who scored the first goal of the 1986 World Cup final between Argentina and West Germany?

400.   Which nation did Argentina defeat in the 1986 World Cup Semi-final?

DIEGO MARADONA

401. What is Diego Maradona's middle name?

402. What year was Diego Maradona born?

403. What Argentinian club did Diego Maradona leave to join Barcelona in 1982?

404. In what year did Diego Maradona win his first Argentinian cap?

405. How much did Barcelona pay to sign Diego Maradona in 1982?

406. What club did Diego Maradona make the most appearances for in his career?

407. In how many World Cup finals tournaments did Diego Maradona play?

408. Against which nation did Diego Maradona score his first goal in World Cup finals?

409. Against which nation did Diego Maradona score his last goal in World Cup finals?

410. What World Cup finals appearance record does Diego Maradona hold?

GARY LINEKER

411. For what club was Gary Lineker playing when he made his World Cup finals debut?

412. What is Gary Lineker's middle name?

413. Which club did Gary Lineker play the most games for in his career?

414. Which member of The Spice Girls is Gary Lineker related to?

415. How many goals did Gary Lineker score in all World Cup finals tournaments?

416. Gary Lineker is England's second top goal scorer in history with how many goals?

417. At which Japanese club did Gary Lineker end his career?

418. What children's television character did Gary Lineker provide the voice for?

419. In what year did Gary Lineker join Tottenham Hotspur?

420. Which Premiership footballer once sued Gary Lineker for defamation following an article in the Sunday Telegraph?

SIR BOBBY ROBSON

421.   In what year was Sir Bobby Robson born?

422.   At which club did Bobby Robson start his professional playing career?

423.   In what year did Bobby Robson win his last England cap?

424.   Name the three English clubs that Bobby Robson has managed.

425.   Which club did Bobby Robson make the most appearances for as a player?

426.   In how many World Cup finals tournaments was Bobby Robson involved in as a player and as a manager?

427.   Bobby Robson's statue stands outside which football ground?

428.   In what year did Bobby Robson win the UEFA Cup as a manager?

429.   Name the four European clubs that Bobby Robson has managed (not including English clubs).

430.   What Canadian club did Bobby Robson play for at the end of his career?

JOSÉ LUIS BROWN

431.   At which club did José Luis Brown make his professional debut?

432.   What year did José Luis Brown make his debut for Argentina?

433.   What was José Luis Brown's nickname?

434.   How many international goals did José Luis Brown score in his career?

435.   Which Spanish club did José Luis Brown play for in 1987-88?

436.   What nationality is Stade Brestois 29, the club that José Luis Brown played for in 1986-87?

437.   At which club did José Luis Brown end his playing career in 1989?

438.   What is the name of the Colombian club that José Luis Brown played for?

439.   Who was the Argentinian coach who allowed José Luis Brown to continue playing in the 1986 World Cup final after he injured his arm?

440.   What year was José Luis Brown born?

PETER SHILTON

441.   How many England caps did Peter Shilton win in total?

442.   How old was Peter Shilton when he made his first appearance
        in a World Cup finals tournament? A: 22, B: 27, C: 32, D: 37.

443.   Peter Shilton jointly holds the World Cup finals record for
        matches without conceding any goals. How many clean sheets
        did he achieve?

444.   Peter Shilton shares the World Cup finals record for matches
        without conceding any goals with which other goalkeeper?

445.   Peter Shilton signed for three clubs and never made
        appearances for them, which clubs?

446.   In how many World Cup finals tournament matches did Peter
        Shilton play?

447.   At which club did Peter Shilton make his 1000th competitive
        appearance?

448.   Peter Shilton was League Runner-up twice in his career one
        with Nottingham Forest in 1979 and with what other club?

449.   Which of the following competitions did Peter Shilton never
        win? A: Division One Championship, B: FA Cup, C: League Cup,
        D: European Champions Cup.

450.   Which of the following clubs did Peter Shilton make the least
        appearances for? A: Leicester City, B: Stoke City, C:
        Nottingham Forest, D: Derby County.

ITALY 1990

451.　Who scored the first goal of the 1990 World Cup finals?

452.　When the Republic of Ireland beat Romania 5-4 on penalties, which player scored the decisive spot kick?

453.　Which nation knocked the World Cup hosts, Italy out in the 1990 semi-final?

454.　Who was top scorer in the 1990 World Cup finals?

455.　Who scored West Germany's winning goal in the 1990 World Cup final against Argentina?

456.　Which nation finished in fourth place in the 1990 World Cup?

457.　Republic of Ireland reached the 1990 World Cup quarter-final, how many tournament goals did they score to get there? A: 1, B: 2, C: 3, D: 4.

458.　Who scored England's winning goal against Egypt in group F?

459.　Who was West Germany's top goal scorer in the 1990 World Cup finals?

460.　Which African player scored 4 goals in the 1990 World Cup finals?

PAULO MALDINI

461. In what year did Paulo Maldini make his debut for Italy?

462. Which club did Paulo Maldini play over 600 games for?

463. In what year did Paulo Maldini become the first defender to win the World Player of the Year award?

464. How many appearances did Paulo Maldini make for Italy? A: 126, B: 131, C: 136, D: 141.

465. Paulo Maldini won the European Cup/Champions League for the fifth time in 2007. What year did he first win the trophy?

466. What is the name of Paulo Maldini's father who picked him for the national team?

467. In what year did Paulo Maldini retire from international football?

468. What was Paulo Maldini best achievement with Italy in any World Cup finals tournament?

469. In 2007 how many seasons had Paulo Maldini completed in Serie A?

470. In how many European Cup / Champions League finals has Paulo Maldini played?

JÜRGEN KLINSMANN

471.   In what year was Jürgen Klinsmann born?

472.   Which club did Jürgen Klinsmann play the most games for in his career?

473.   In what year did Jürgen Klinsmann make his debut for West Germany?

474.   How many goals did Jürgen Klinsmann score in World Cup finals tournaments?

475.   What colour medal did Jürgen Klinsmann win at the 1988 Olympic Games?

476.   What club did Jürgen Klinsmann join when he left Tottenham Hotspur in 1995?

477.   In what year did Jürgen Klinsmann become the German national head coach?

478.   Which Italian club did Jürgen Klinsmann play for?

479.   In what year did Jürgen Klinsmann win the European Championship with Germany?

480.   What is the name of the first professional club that Jürgen Klinsmann played for?

RUDI VÖLLER

481. In what year was Rudi Völler born?

482. In which World Cup tournament did Rudi Völler coach Germany?

483. How many World Cup finals tournaments did Rudi Völler play in?

484. Which club was Rudi Völler playing for when he made his international debut?

485. Which Italian club did Rudi Völler play for between 1987 and 1992?

486. With which club did Rudi Völler win the European cup in 1993?

487. With which club did Rudi Völler finish his playing career?

488. Rudi Völler was once sent off with a Dutch player in a World Cup match, name the player that spat at Völler.

489. Which club did Rudi Völler join in 1980?

490. In what year did Rudi Völler last play for Germany?

TOTÒ SCHILLACI

491. What was Totò Schillaci's real name?

492. What club was Totò Schillaci playing for when he made his debut for Italy?

493. How many goals did Totò Schillaci in Italia 90?

494. Which club did Totò Schillaci make 219 appearances for between 1982 and 1989?

495. In what year was Totò Schillaci born?

496. Who was the Italian coach who selected Totò Schillaci for the 1990 World Cup squad?

497. Against which nation did Totò Schillaci score his first goal in the 1990 World Cup finals tournament?

498. Against which nation did Totò Schillaci score his sixth and final goal of the 1990 World Cup?

499. How many international caps did Totò Schillaci win in his career? A: 16, B: 26, C: 36 D: 46.

500. In what country did Totò Schillaci play out the last three years of his professional career?

PAUL GASCOIGNE

501. In which town was Paul Gascoigne born?

502. Which manager gave Paul Gascoigne his Newcastle United debut?

503. Against which nation did Paul Gascoigne make his international debut?

504. Which club did Paul Gascoigne sign for in 2000?

505. Which German player did Paul Gascoigne foul when he received his yellow card in the 1990 World Cup semi-final?

506. With which club did Paul Gascoigne win two domestic league championships?

507. What year did Paul Gascoigne win the BBC Sports Personality of the Year award?

508. In how many World Cup finals tournaments did Paul Gascoigne play?

509. In the 1991 FA Cup final Paul Gascoigne ruptured his cruciate ligaments after fouling which Nottingham Forest player?

510. Which Football League club did Paul Gascoigne play six games for in 2002?

USA 1994

511.   Which two players shared the top goal scorer in the 1994 World Cup finals?

512.   Who scored the first goal of the 1994 World Cup finals?

513.   Which Colombian defender was murdered when he returned home from the 1994 World Cup after he scored an own goal against the USA that eliminated his team?

514.   Which referee represented the absent England in the 1994 World Cup finals?

515.   Which Russian scored five goals in the 6-1 win against Cameroon in the 1994 World Cup finals?

516.   Which European nation left the 1994 World Cup finals without scoring a single goal?

517.   Who scored the Republic of Ireland's winning goal against the eventual losing 1994 World Cup finalists, Italy?

518.   What was so special about the USA's 1994 World Cup final match against Switzerland at the Pontiac Silverdome?

519.   Which nation finished third in the 1994 World Cup?

520.   Which Italian player's missed penalty handed the 1994 World Cup to Brazil?

DUNGA

521. What is Dunga's real name?

522. Which Italian football club did Dunga join in 1987?

523. What colour medal did Dunga win at the 1984 Olympic Games?

524. How many World Cup finals tournaments did Dunga play in?

525. In what year did Dunga win his first cap with Brazil?

526. In what year did Dunga become manager of Brazil?

527. Which European club did Dunga make the most appearances for?

528. In what country was Dunga playing club football when he played in the 1998 World Cup finals?

529. Which English club is Dunga a co-owner/director of?

530. What is the English translation of the Portugese word dunga?

ROMÁRIO

531. What is Romário's real name?

532. In what year was Romário born?

533. At which club did Romário begin his professional career?

534. Which club did Romário play the most games for in his career?

535. What year did Romário make his Brazilian debut?

536. In which year did Romário win an Olympic Silver Medal?

537. In how many World Cup finals tournaments did Romário play?

538. In what year did Romário play his last game for Brazil?

539. For which club was Romário playing for when he scored what he claims was the 1000th goal of his career in May 2007?

540. Romário was part of the famous Ro-Ro forward line for Brazil, who was the other player in the partnership?

ROBERTO BAGGIO

541. In what year was Roberto Baggio born?

542. At which club did Roberto Baggio begin his professional career?

543. What year did Roberto Baggio win his first Italian cap?

544. In how many World Cup finals tournaments did Roberto Baggio play?

545. In what year did Roberto Baggio win the World Player of the Year award?

546. Which of Roberto Baggio's brothers was also a professional footballer?

547. Which Italian sportswear company was Roberto Baggio associated with most during his career?

548. Roberto Baggio was born into the Catholic faith. What religion did he convert to?

549. Which club did Roberto Baggio play the most games for during his career?

550. At which club did Roberto Baggio end his playing career in 2004?

FRANCE 1998

551.   Who scored the first goal of the 1998 World Cup finals?

552.   Which of the 1998 World Cup stadiums had the largest capacity?

553.   Which Argentinean striker scored a hat trick in his nation's 5-0 victory against Jamaica in Group H of the 1998 World Cup?

554.   Who was the top goal scorer in the 1998 World Cup finals?

555.   Which referee represented England in the 1998 World Cup finals?

556.   Who scored USA's only goal of the 1998 World Cup finals?

557.   Who scored both of France's goal in their 2-1 World Cup 1998 semi-final victory against Croatia?

558.   Which Italian player scored five goals during the 1998 World Cup finals?

559.   Which player was France's top goal scorer in the 1998 World Cup finals with 3 goals?

560.   Which nation shared the FIFA Fair Play trophy with France in the 1998 World Cup finals?

ZINEDINE ZIDANE

561.   Where was Zinedine Zidane born?

562.   At which club did Zinedine Zidane begin his professional career?

563.   Which club did Zinedine Zidane leave when he joined Juventus in 1996?

564.   In which year did Zinedine Zidane make his debut for France?

565.   From which nation did Zinedine Zidane's parents immigrate?

566.   Who was the Italian player that Zinedine Zidane head-butted in the chest in the 2006 World Cup final?

567.   On how many occasions did Zinedine Zidane win the World Player of the Year Award?

568.   How many caps did Zinedine Zidane win with France? A: 93, B: 98, C: 103, D: 108.

569.   Which club did Zinedine Zidane play the most competitive matches for?

570.   How many times did Zinedine Zidane win the UEFA Champions League?

DAVID BECKHAM (PART 1)

571. What are David Beckham's middle names?

572. In what year did David Beckham win the PFA Young Player of the Year award?

573. In what year did David Beckham marry Spice Girl, Victoria Adams?

574. In what year did David Beckham win the BBC Sports Personality of the Year?

575. Against which nation did David Beckham make his England debut?

576. In what year did David Beckham become England captain?

577. Against which club did David Beckham break his metatarsal bone?

578. David Beckham claimed that his performance against Greece in the final World Cup qualifier of 2001 was inspired by the mascot for the day. What is the name of the little girl that Beckham also helped to escort the Jubilee Baton to Her Majesty the Queen at the 2002 Commonwealth Games in 2002?

579. How many English Premiership and La Liga titles did David Beckham win during his career with Manchester United and Real Madrid?

580. Who did David Beckham replace as England Captain?

MICHAEL OWEN

581. In what year did Michael Owen win the European Footballer of the Year Award?

582. In what year did Michael Owen make his debut for Liverpool?

583. Against which nation, in the 2006 World Cup finals did Michael Owen seriously injure his right knee, sidelining him for nearly a year?

584. Against which nation did Michael Owen win his first England cap, making him the youngest player to represent the full England team?

585. Against which nation did Michael Owen score his first goal in a World Cup finals tournament in 1998?

586. In what year did Michael Owen win the BBC Sport Personality of the Year award?

587. In which two consecutive seasons was Michael Owen the English Premier League's top goal scorer?

588. In what year did Michael Owen help Liverpool to win the League Cup, FA Cup and UEFA Cup?

589. Against which nation did Michael Owen score his first post World Cup 2006 goal for England?

590. In which English city was Michael Owen born?

RONALDO

591.   What is Ronaldo's full name?

592.   Which club did Ronaldo leave to join Barcelona in 1996?

593.   In what year did Ronaldo win his first cap for Brazil?

594.   What name did Ronaldo wear on his shirt when he played in the 1996 Olympic Games?

595.   Against which nation did Ronaldo score his first goal in World Cup finals?

596.   Which club was Ronaldo with when he missed the whole of the 2000-01 season due to injury?

597.   Against which nation, in the 2006 World Cup finals, did Ronaldo score the goal that broke Gerd Muller's World Cup finals scoring record of 14 goals?

598.   What club did Ronaldo join when he left Real Madrid in 2007?

599.   Ronaldo is co-owner of the Brazilian A1 Motor Racing team. Which racing legend also owns the team?

600.   How many goals did Ronaldo score in the 2002 World Cup finals?

HENRIK LARSSON

601.   What club did Henrik Larsson leave to join Celtic in 1997?

602.   Where in Sweden was Henrik Larsson born?

603.   In what year did Henrik Larsson win his first Swedish cap?

604.   Against which nation did Henrik Larsson score his first World Cup finals goal in 1994?

605.   How many goals did Henrik Larsson score in all of the World Cup finals tournaments he played in?

606.   Against which nation did Henrik Larsson play his last World Cup match?

607.   How many Scottish Premier League titles did Henrik Larsson win with Celtic?

608.   What national honour did the UK bestow upon Henrik Larsson in 2006?

609.   Which of the following medals did Henrik Larsson not win during his career? A: UEFA Champions League, B: English Premier League, C: UEFA Cup, D: Swedish Cup.

610.   How many Spanish League titles did Henrik Larsson win?

RONALDINHO

611.   From what club did Barcelona sign Ronaldinho in 2003?

612.   In what year did Ronaldinho make his full debut for Brazil?

613.   What is Ronaldinho's full name?

614.   Who were the other two members of the famed Three Rs in the 2002 World Cup finals, along with Ronaldinho?

615.   In the 2002 World Cup Quarter Final match against England. Ronaldinho scored and then was sent off for a foul against which player?

616.   How many goals did Ronaldinho score in the 2002 and 2006 World Cup finals combined?

617.   How many times had Ronaldinho won the FIFA World Player of the year award as of 2006?

618.   In what year did Ronaldinho first win the European Champions League?

619.   In what year was Ronaldinho born?

620.   At what Brazilian club did Ronaldinho begin his professional career?

MIROSLAV KLOSE

621.   In what country was Miroslav Klose born?

622.   For what club was Miroslav Klose playing for when he made his international debut?

623.   How many goals did Miroslav Klose score in the 2002 and 2006 World Cup finals combined?

624.   Miroslav Klose scored a hat-trick on his World Cup finals debut, against which nation?

625.   What club did Miroslav Klose join in 2004?

626.   In what year did Miroslav Klose win the German Footballer of the Year award?

627.   What club did Miroslav Klose join in 2007?

628.   Against which nation did Miroslav Klose score his last goal of the 2006 World Cup?

629.   What did all five of Miroslav Klose's 2002 World Cup finals goals all have in common?

630.   What is Miroslav Klose's 'trademark' goal celebration, which he did five times in the 2002 World Cup finals?

DAVID SEAMAN

631. Which club did David Seaman make his professional debut for?

632. Which World Cup final's tournament was David Seaman an unused squad member?

633. What competition did David Seaman win with England in 1997?

634. How many English league titles did David Seaman win with Arsenal?

635. If you add David Seaman and Peter Shilton's England caps together, what is the total?

636. How many FA Cup winner's medals did David Seaman receive?

637. Against which nation did David Seaman make his World Cup finals' debut?

638. How many appearances did David Seaman make for Arsenal? A: 305, B: 355, C: 405, D: 455.

639. In what year was David Seaman awarded an MBE for services to sport?

640. In what year did David Seaman win his first England cap?

FABIEN BARTHEZ

641.   What is Fabien Barthez's middle name?

642.   At which club did Fabien Barthez begin his professional career?

643.   In what year did Fabien Barthez win his first French cap?

644.   What club did Fabien Barthez leave to join Manchester United?

645.   Which French defender used to kiss Fabien Barthez on the head before every match?

646.   With which club did Fabien Barthez win the European Champions League?

647.   How many Premier League titles did Fabien Barthez win with Manchester United?

648.   What record does Fabien Barthez hold in regards to World Cup matches against Brazil?

649.   What club did Fabien Barthez join in 2006?

650.   How many goals did Fabien Barthez concede in the 1998 World Cup finals?

MICHAEL BALLACK

651. In what year was Michael Ballack born?

652. At what club did Michael Ballack begin his professional career?

653. In what year did Michael Ballack win his first German cap?

654. What club did Michael Ballack leave when he joined Bayern Munich in 2002?

655. What nation was Germany playing when Michael Ballack won his first cap?

656. How much did Chelsea pay Bayern Munich for Michael Ballack's services?

657. Against which nation did Michael Ballack score his first World Cup finals tournament goal?

658. How many goals did Michael Ballack score in the 2006 World Cup finals tounament?

659. What shirt number does Michael Ballack prefer to wear when he plays?

660. Against which German club did Michael Ballack score his first goal for Chelsea?

DENNIS BERGKAMP

661. At which club did Dennis Bergkamp begin his professional career?

662. What player was Dennis Bergkamp named after?

663. What year did Dennis Bergkamp join Arsenal?

664. What year did Dennis Bergkamp win his first Dutch cap?

665. Against which nation did Dennis Bergkamp score his first goal in World Cup finals tournaments?

666. Dennis Bergkamp scored his last World Cup finals goal in the 1998 quarter final against which nation?

667. In what year did Dennis Bergkamp retire from international football?

668. In what year did Dennis Bergkamp win the English PFA's Players' Player of the Year award?

669. What prevented Dennis Bergkamp from playing matches for Arsenal outside Britain?

670. What nickname did Dennis Bergkamp earn in regard to question 669?

KOREA/JAPAN 2002

671. Which referee represented England in the 2002 World Cup finals?

672. Who scored the first goal of the 2002 World Cup finals?

673. Three nations left the 2002 World Cup without scoring a goal. China, Saudi Arabia and which other country?

674. Ronaldo won the Golden Boot for the 2002 World Cup finals after scoring 8 goals. Who finished in joint second place alongside Miroslav Klose?

675. Which Asian nation won Group D in the 2002 World Cup finals?

676. Which Irish player scored three goals during the 2002 World Cup finals?

677. Which nation did Brazil knock out in the Semi-finals of the 2002 World Cup?

678. Which nation did Germany knock out in the Semi-final of the 2002 World Cup?

679. Which nation did USA beat to progress to the World Cup Quarter-finals of 2002?

680. Who scored England's last goal of the 2002 World Cup finals?

RIVALDO

681. What is Rivaldo's real name?

682. What was the first European club that Rivaldo signed for in 1996?

683. Which club did Rivaldo play the most games for in his career?

684. In what year did Rivaldo win the UEFA Champions League?

685. Against which nation did Rivaldo score his first World Cup finals goal?

686. How many goals did Rivaldo score in the two World Cup finals tournaments that he played in?

687. What Greek club did Rivaldo join in 2004?

688. Which club did Rivaldo join when he left Barcelona in 2002?

689. Which Greek club did Rivaldo join in 2007?

690. In what year did Rivaldo win the FIFA World Player of the Year award?

ROBERTO CARLOS

691.   What is Roberto Carlos's full name?

692.   In 2007 Roberto Carlos left Real Madrid to join which club?

693.   Against which nation did Roberto Carlos score his one and only goal in World Cup finals?

694.   In which World Cup finals did Roberto Carlos first play in?

695.   How many times did Roberto Carlos win the UEFA Champions League?

696.   Which club did Roberto Carlos leave to join Real Madrid in 1996?

697.   Against which nation did Roberto Carlos play his last game for Brazil in the 2006 World Cup finals?

698.   How many La Liga titles did Roberto Carlos win with Real Madrid?

699.   Roberto Carlos won a Bronze Medal at which year's Olympic Games?

700.   How many times did Roberto Carlos win the Copa del Rey with Real Madrid?

ALESSANDRO DEL PIERO

701.   In what year was Alessandro Del Piero born.

702.   At which club did Alessandro Del Piero begin his professional career?

703.   In what year did Alessandro Del Piero make his international debut?

704.   Against which nation did Alessandro Del Piero score his first goal in World Cup finals?

705.   What role did Alessandro Del Piero have in the 2006 Winter Olympic Games in Turin?

706.   In the 2006 World Cup finals match against Germany Alessandro Del Piero set a new record when he scored, what record was that?

707.   Alessandro Del Piero was the UEFA Champions League top scorer in two consecutive years, which ones?

708.   What record does Alessandro Del Piero hold with Juventus?

709.   In what year did Alessandro Del Piero win the UEFA Champions League?

710.   What club did Alessandro Del Piero's older brother, Stefano briefly play for?

RAÚL

711.   What is Raúl's real name?

712.   At which club did Raúl make his La Liga debut?

713.   In what year did Raúl make his La Liga debut?

714.   What UEFA Champions League first did Raúl achieve 28th September 2005 when he scored against Olympiakos?

715.   Against which nation did Raúl score his first goal in World Cup finals?

716.   How many goals has Raúl scored in the 3 World Cup finals tournaments that he has played in?

717.   What international goal scoring record did Raúl hold in 2008?

718.   Raúl named his first son Jorge after one of his former managers at Real Madrid, who?

719.   What number shirt does Raúl wear at Real Madrid?

720.   What year did Raúl become captain of the Spanish national team?

LUÍS FIGO

721. In what year was Luís Figo born?

722. In what Portugese city was Luís Figo born?

723. At which club did Luís Figo make professional debut?

724. What club did Luís Figo leave to join Real Madrid in 2000?

725. In what year did Luís Figo make his international debut?

726. How many goals has Luís Figo scored in World Cup finals tournaments?

727. How many caps did Luís Figo win with Portugal? A: 127, B: 128, C: 129, D: 130.

728. What is Luís Figo's preferred shirt number?

729. In what year did Luís Figo win the FIFA World Player of the Year award?

730. What club did Luís Figo join in 2005?

DAVID BECKHAM (PART 2)

731. What is the name of David Beckham's last manager at Real Madrid?

732. Why did the World's paparazzi agree not to take any photographs of David Beckham's son, Romeo?

733. David Beckham is the first Englishman to do what in three different World Cup finals tournaments?

734. David Beckham suffers from OCD, what do those initials stand for?

735. David Beckham was dropped by which advertiser when he first shaved his head?

736. What year was the film Bend it like Beckham released?

737. After David Beckham's sending off against Argentina in the 1998 World Cup finals, which English newspaper published a dartboard with Beckham's face in the middle?

738. Which two consecutive years was David Beckham runner up for the World Footballer of the Year award?

739. In what year was David Beckham awarded the OBE by Her Majesty The Queen?

740. How many times was David Beckham sent off while playing for Real Madrid?

GERMANY 2006

741. Who scored the first goal of the 2006 World Cup finals?

742. Who scored Italy's last minute goal that knocked Australia out of the Round of 16 stage of the 2006 World Cup finals?

743. Which nation did Brazil knock out of the Round of 16 stage of the 2006 World Cup finals?

744. Which nation knocked Holland out of the 2006 World Cup finals?

745. Who was the only England player to score a penalty in the World Cup 2006 Quarter-final shootout against Portugal?

746. Who scored the goal that knocked Brazil out of the 2006 World Cup finals?

747. Who scored Italy's second goal in the World Cup semi-final against Germany?

748. Who scored France's winner in the World Cup semi-final against Portugal?

749. Which French player missed his penalty in the World Cup final shootout against Italy?

750. English referee Graham Poll controversially booked which player three times in one match?

THIERRY HENRY

751. At which club did Thierry Henry make his professional debut?

752. In what year did Thierry Henry make international debut?

753. How much did Arsenal pay Juventus when they signed Thierry Henry in 1999?

754. What is the name of the manager who gave Thierry Henry his debut in the French league?

755. Arsenal signed Thierry Henry as a replacement for which of his French international team mates?

756. How many times was Thierry Henry the English Premier League's top goal scorer?

757. What is Thierry Henry's middle name?

758. Who was the French national coach who gave Thierry Henry his first cap?

759. How much did Barcelona pay Arsenal when they signed Thierry Henry in 2007?

760. What is the name of Thierry Henry's estranged wife with whom he had a highly publicised, bitter separation from in 2007?

TRIVIA

761. Who is fourth in the all-time World Cup finals top scorer list?

762. Which English player has scored the second most goals for his country in World Cup finals?

763. Which German international has appeared in 5 different World Cup finals Tournaments?

764. Who is the only national head coach to have won the World Cup twice?

765. The referee added on 8 minutes of injury time to the first half of extra-time in the 1990 Semi-Final between Italy and Argentina, why? A: He forgot to check his watch, B: An Argentinean player was knocked unconscious, C: There was a pitch invasion, D: The referee was injured.

766. What happened to Italy's Gianfranco Zola when he played a World Cup 1994 finals match on his 28th Birthday? A: He scored his first World Cup goal, B: He broke his toe, C: He missed two penalties, D: He was sent off.

767. Why was the kick-off of the 1974 World Cup final delayed?

768. Who was the first goalkeeper ever to be sent off in a World Cup finals match in 1994?

769. Lucien Laurent of France is the first player to do what?

770. Who are the only twin brothers to have scored in a World Cup finals tournament?

OLIVER KAHN

771. What club did Oliver Kahn leave when he joined Bayern Munich in 1994?

772. In what year did Oliver Kahn make his international debut?

773. Oliver Kahn spent the whole of the 1998 World Cup finals on the substitutes bench, who was the goalkeeper that kept Kahn out of the team?

774. Who was the goalkeeper that kept Oliver Kahn out of the German team for most of the 2006 World Cup finals tournament?

775. What award did Oliver Kahn earn because of his performances at the 2002 World Cup finals?

776. As of 2007, how many Bundesliga titles has Oliver Kahn won with Bayern Munich?

777. In what year did Oliver Kahn first win the UEFA Champions League?

778. What international winners' medal does Oliver Kahn have?

779. What was the title of Oliver Kahn's autobiography?

780. How many international caps had Kahn earned with Germany by the end of 2006? A: 86, B: 96, C: 106, D: 116.

MARTIN PETERS MBE

781.   In what year was Martin Peters born?

782.   What year did Martin Peters make his international debut?

783.   What club did Martin Peters play the most games for in his career?

784.   What year did Martin Peters make his professional first team debut?

785.   What club did Martin Peters join when he left Tottenham Hotspur in 1975?

786.   Against which nation did Martin Peters make his England debut?

787.   When Martin Peters joined Tottenham Hotspur in 1970 which player went in the opposite way as part of the transfer deal?

788.   Which of the six 1966 World Cup finals goals did Martin Peters score? (1st, 2nd, 3rd, 4th, 5th or 6th).

789.   At what club did Martin Peters end his playing career?

790.   Against which nation did Martin Peters score his last goal in World Cup finals (1970)?

MORE TRIVIA

791. Where was Croatian international defender Josip Šimuni? born?

792. What World Cup finals record does Turkey's Lefter Kucukandonyadis hold?

793. Who is the oldest player to have played in a World Cup finals game (as of 2006)?

794. Who is the youngest player to have played in a World Cup finals game (as of 2006)?

795. Which player has completed the most matches (played the whole game) in World Cup finals tournaments?

796. Which player has played in the most World Cup final ties (the final itself)?

797. Which player has played in the most World Cup finals matches as captain?

798. Who is the only player to have scored in consecutive World Cup final ties?

799. Who is the only player to have scored a hat trick in consecutive World Cup tournaments?

800. Who was the first player to score a 'Golden Goal' in a World Cup finals tournament?

LOTHAR MATTHÄUS

801. At which club did Lothar Matthäus begin his professional career?

802. How many German caps did Lothar Matthäus win in his career? (Clue: The figure ends with a zero).

803. Which club did Lothar Matthäus play for in between two spells with Bayern Munich?

804. In what year did Lothar Matthäus win his first German cap?

805. In what year did Lothar Matthäus win the European Footballer of the Year award?

806. Which national team did Lothar Matthäus manage between 2003 and 2005?

807. Against which nation did Lothar Matthäus score his first goal in World Cup finals tournaments?

808. In what year did Lothar Matthäus win the World Player of the Year award?

809. Lothar Matthäus played his last match for Germany in Euro 90 against which nation?

810. What was the first club to employ Lothar Matthäus as a coach?

GABRIEL BATISTUTA

811.   What was the first European club that Gabriel Batistuta played for?

812.   In what year did Gabriel Batistuta make his international debut?

813.   When Fiorentina were relegated to serie B in 1993, where did Gabriele Batistuta go?

814.   Against which nation did Gabriel Batistuta score his first World Cup finals goal?

815.   How many goals did Gabriel Batistuta score in all of the World Cup finals tournaments he played in, in total?

816.   Which former Argentinian captain was Gabriel Batistuta's coach when he was playing for River Plate?

817.   Who was Gabriel Batistuta's coach between 1993 and 1997?

818.   How many goals did Gabriel Basitstuta score for Argentina in 78 games? A: 36, B: 46 C: 56, D: 66.

819.   Which club did Gabriel Batistuta join when he left AS Roma in 2003?

820.   Against which nation did Gabriel Batistuta play his last game for Argentina?

ZICO

821. Which Italian club did Zico play for?

822. Which club did Zico play the most games for in his career?

823. Which nation was Zico the head coach for at the 2006 World Cup finals?

824. In which year did Zico make his international debut with Brazil?

825. Against which South American nation did Zico score his first World Cup finals goal in 1978?

826. How many goals did Zico score in the three World Cup finals tournaments he played in?

827. In 1995 Zico became a World Champion with Brazil in which sport?

828. In which year did Zico play his last game for Brazil?

829. Which one of the following, are the correct appearance and goals stats for Zico with Brazil? A: 77 games 44 goals, B: 88 games 66 goals, C: 99 games 55 goals, D: 77 games 33 goals.

830. Against which nation did Zico score his last World Cup finals goal?

BRAZIL TRIVIA

831. In what year did Rivelino make his debut for Brazil?

832. Which English non-league club did Sócrates play one league game for in 2004?

833. The Brazilian national team is generally considered to have played their first match against which English club in 1914?

834. Brazil's biggest ever defeat was by 6-0 in 1920 to which nation?

835. Who scored Brazil's first ever goal in the World Cup finals of 1930?

836. Name the five years in which Brazil has won the World Cup.

837. Who are the top three top goal scorers of all time for Brazil?

838. Against which nation did Brazil inflict their biggest ever victory (14-0) in 1975?

839. How many times had Brazil appeared in World Cup finals when they competed in the 2006 World Cup finals?

840. When Brazil won the Copa America in 2007, how many times had the won the competition in total?

CAFU

841. What is Cafu's full name?

842. What Spanish club did Cafu play for in 1995?

843. What Brazilian international record did Cafu hold in 2007?

844. What club did Cafu join in 2003?

845. As of 2007, which club had Cafu played the most games for?

846. In what year did Cafu win his first Brazilian cap in a friendly against Spain?

847. Cafu speaks Portuguese and which other two languages?

848. Cafu's squad number was 2 in his last World Cup finals tournament, but what shirt did he wear in his first?

849. At which Brazilian club did Cafu begin his professional career?

850. In what year was Cafu born?

ALAN SHEARER

851. As a schoolboy, Alan Shearer was rejected by Newcastle United after an unsuccessful trial in what position?

852. What record did Alan Shearer set when he scored a hat trick against Arsenal for Southampton on 9th April 1988?

853. Against which nation did Alan Shearer make his goal scoring England debut in 1992?

854. When Alan Shearer was at Blackburn Rovers he was a member of a prolific striking partnership. Who was the other member of the SAS?

855. Against which nation did Alan Shearer score his first goal in World Cup finals?

856. How many goals did Alan Shearer score in all of the World Cup tournaments he played in?

857. Against which nation did Alan Shearer score his last international goal?

858. Alan Shearer only ever scored one international hat trick. Against which nation was that?

859. When Alan Shearer retired from playing in 2006 he was the English Premier League's all time top goal scorer. How many goals did he score?

860. In what year did Alan Shearer pick up an English Premier League winners medal?

TRIVIA RETURNS

861. Who is the only player to have played World Cup qualifying football and World Cup cricket?

862. The World Cup match that attracted the largest ever attendance was a game between Brazil and Uruguay. 200,000 spectators turned up but in what year was the match played?

863. Why was the World Cup match between England and Brazil in 1962 interrupted?

864. In what year was the tradition of swapping shirts introduced to the World Cup finals?

865. Which was the first black African nation to compete in a World Cup finals tournament?

866. In the World Cup of 1982 the President of Kuwaiti walked onto the pitch and successfully persuaded the referee to disallow a goal scored by their opponents that day, France. What argument did the President use to change the referee's mind?

867. In the 1982 World Cup semi final between West Germany and France the German goal keeper, Harald Schumacher made an infamous challenge, seriously injuring which French player?

868. What did an Iraqi defender do to a referee in the 1986 World Cup which resulted in him receiving a one year ban? A: He spat at him, B: He pushed him to the ground, C: He punched him, D: He racially abused him.

869. Who are the only brothers to have managed the same nation in the history of the World Cup?

870. The match between Italy and Spain in the 1934 World Cup was the first what?

PATRICK VIEIRA

871.   At which club did Patrick Vieira begin his professional career?

872.   In which nation was Patrick Vieira born?

873.   At which club was Patrick Vieira playing when he won his first French cap?

874.   If you added all of Patrick Vieira's English Premiership and FA Cup winners medals, how many would there be?

875.   Against which nation did Patrick Vieira make his international debut?

876.   How many goals in total has Patrick Vieira score in the three World Cup finals tournaments he has played in?

877.   In what year did Patrick Vieira make his debut for Juventus?

878.   What was Patrick Vieira's shirt number at Internazionale (Inter Milan)?

879.   What club did Arsenal sign Patrick Vieira from?

880.   Patrick Vieira was a Championship winner and relegated in the same season, how?

ITALY

881. In what year did the Italian national team play its first competitive match?

882. Which nation inflicted Italy's biggest ever defeat (7-2) in 1924?

883. Which player scored Italy's first ever goal in World Cup finals and a hat trick in the same match in 1934? A: Raimundo Orsi, B: Angelo Schiavio, C: Giuseppe Meazza, D: Giovanni Ferrari.

884. What nickname do members of the Italian team collectively have?

885. Which year did Italy fail to qualify for the World Cup finals?

886. As of 2007, who was Italy's all time top goal scorer with 35 goals?

887. Which Italian club has had at least one player in the Italian World Cup squad since 1934?

888. Which player scored two goals for Italy in the 1938 World Cup final and also holds the record of the highest goal scorer in Italian Serie A history?

889. In what year did the Italy football team win the Olympic gold medal?

890. Which nation caused a shock when they beat Italy 1-0 in the 1966 World Cup finals?

URUGUAY 1930 REVISITED

891. The first two World Cup matches took place simultaneously and were won by which two nations?

892. How many goals were scored in the 1930 World Cup finals? A: 50, B: 60, C: 70 D: 80.

893. What was the main reason the World Cup was initiated?

894. Uruguay, Argentina, Brazil and which other nation was seeded for the 1930 World Cup finals?

895. In Group 1 France faced Argentina in the 1930 World Cup Argentina were 1-0 up when the first incident of refereeing controversy occurred. Was it A: France was awarded an equaliser when the ball entered the back of the net through the side netting? B: An Argentinean player was sent off after an incident of mistaken identity? C: The referee blew for time six minutes early only to be persuaded later to play on? D: The referee added on ten minutes when his watch stopped, allowing the French to score twice and win the game?

896. In the 1930 World Cup finals group 2 match between Brazil and Bolivia there was a considerable amount of confusion for 45 minutes, why?

897. What milestone in World Cup history is connected with Plácido Galindo of Peru when he played in the 1930 World Cup match between Peru and Romania?

898. As of August 2007, Francisco Varallo was the last surviving player from the 1930 World Cup final. What nation did he play for?

899. Who was the top goal scorer in the 1930 World Cup finals? A: Bert Patenaude, B: Pedro Cea, C: Guillermo Subiabre, D: Guillermo Stábile.

900. Which nation departed the 1930 World Cup after having conceded 8 goals and scoring none?

ITALY 1934 REVISETED

901.   In the 1934 World Cup the World Champions Uruguay did not participate, why?

902.   Which of the following four players finished as top goal scorer in the 1934 Word Cup? A: Oldřich Nejedlý, B: Edmund Conen, C: Angelo Schiavio, D: Raimundo Orsi.

903.   How many goals were scored in the whole of the 1934 World Cup finals tournament? A: 50, B: 60, C: 70, D: 80.

904.   Who was the Italian leader at the time of the 1934 World Cup?

905.   All of the 1934 World Cup first round matches kicked off at the same time, but who scored the first goal of the finals? A: Sven Jonasson, B: Leopold Kielholz, C: Edmund Conen, D: Ernesto Belis.

906.   Which nation knocked Brazil out of the 1934 World Cup?

907.   One of the 1934 World Cup quarter-finals had to be decided after a replay. Which two nations played in that tie?

908.   Name the four semi-finalist at the 1934 World Cup finals.

909.   Which nation finished third in the 1934 World Cup?

910.   Who scored the winning goal for Italy in the 1934 World Cup final? A: Raimundo Orsi, B: Angelo Schiavio, C: Enrique Guaita, D: Giuseppe Meazza.

FRANCE 1938 REVISITED

911. Who was the top goal scorer at the 1938 World Cup finals?
A: Roberto, B: Romeu, C: Leônidas, D: José Perácio.

912. Which nation knocked the Nazi German team out of the 1938 World Cup finals?

913. Hungary knocked out the Dutch East Indies in the first round of the 1938 World Cup finals. By what name is The Dutch East Indies known now?

914. Who scored the first goal of the 1938 World Cup finals? A: André Abegglen, B: Josef Gauchel, C: Wilhelm Hahnemann, D: Alfed Bickel.

915. Which nation finished third in the 1938 World Cup finals?

916. In their second round match, Sweden's Tore Keller and Gustav Wetterström both scored hat tricks but which one of them completed theirs in the first half?

917. Which nation did Italy defeat in the World Cup second round of 1938? A: Switzerland, B: Cuba, C: France, D: Czechoslovakia.

918. In Brazil's 1938 World Cup match against Poland, Brazilian striker Leônidas decided to play bear foot because of the muddy conditions. What subsequently happened to him in that match? A: He scored four goals, B: He fractured his metatarsal, C: A FIFA Official demanded he put his boots on but Leônidas refused and was technically sent off, D: He broke an opponent's leg in a miss timed challenge.

919. What was Brazil's Leônidas's occupation outside football? A: Policeman, B: Lifeguard, C: Private Investigator, D: Government Secret Agent.

920. Who finished the 1938 World Cup as the second top goal scorer? A: Silvio Piola, B: Gino Colaussi, C: Gyula Zsengellér, D: György Sárosi.

BRAZIL 1950 REVISITED

921. Who was top goal scorer in the 1950 World Cup finals? A: Chico, B: Admir, C: Baltazar, D: Alfredo.

922. India qualified for the 1950 World Cup but refused to participate for what reason? A: They could not afford to travel to Brazil, B: They would not be allowed to play barefoot, C: There were no other Asian nations in the tournament, D: A Brazilian official made an insulting remark prior to the tournament.

923. How many goals were scored in total in the 1950 World Cup finals? A: 68, B: 78, C: 88, D: 98.

924. Who scored the first goal of the 1950 World Cup finals? A: Jair, B: Baltazar, C: Ademir, D: Alfredo.

925. Group 4 of the 1950 World Cup only had two teams in it, therefore one nation departed having only played one game. Which nation was that?

926. The 1950 World Cup final is only regarded as the final because, just by chance, it was the last game in the four nation final pool that decided who was World Champions. Who would have won the tournament if they game had been drawn?

927. Which nation finished third in the 1950 World Cup?

928. Which Spanish player finished as joint second top goal scorer in the 1950 World Cup alongside Oscar Míguez of Uruguay? A: Estanislao Basora, B: Zarra, C: Silvestre Igoa, D: Friaça.

929. Which two nations should have played in Group 4 of the 1950 World Cup but withdrew just before the tournament?

930. Which nation beat Italy in Group 3 of the 1950 World Cup, technically knocking them out of the tournament?

SWITZERLAND
1954 REVISITED

931. Who was the top goal scorer in the 1954 World Cup finals?
A: Eric Probst, B: Max Morlock, C: Sándor Kocsis, D: Ottmar
Walter.

932. Who scored the first goal of the 1954 World Cup finals? A:
Didi, B: Pinga, C: Julinho D: Baltazar.

933. Which nation finished third in the 1954 World Cup finals?

934. In which city was the World Cup final of 1954 played?

935. Which nation knocked England out of the 1954 World Cup?

936. One of the 1954 World Cup quarter-finals ended with a final
score of 7-5. Name one of the teams involved in that match.

937. Who was the top scoring English player in the 1954 World
Cup finals?

938. What was the only quarter-finalist nations not to score a goal
in the 1954 World Cup last eight?

939. Who scored England's last goal of the 1954 World Cup finals?

940. Which nation did West Germany beat 6-1 in the 1954 World
Cup semi-finals?

SWEDEN 1958 REVISITED

941.   Who scored the first goal of the 1958 World Cup finals? A: Nils Liedholm, B: Kurt Hamrin, C: Agne Simonsson, D: Lennart Skoglund.

942.   Who scored Brazil's first goal of the 1958 World Cup finals? A: Didi, B: Pelé, C: Zagallo, D: Mazola.

943.   Who was the first player to score against Brazil in the 1958 World Cup finals?

944.   Which 1966 World Cup finalist scored for West Germany against Argentina in one of the opening matches of Group 1 in the 1958 World Cup finals?

945.   Wales had to compete in a play-off against Hungary to qualify from Group 3 of the 1958 World Cup finals, who scored the winning goal for the Welsh? A: Ivor Allchurch, B: Terry Medwin, C: John Charles, D: Ron Hewitt.

946.   In Group 4 of the 1958 World Cup finals, USSR and England finished after scoring and conceding the same amount of goals and having the same goal average. Why, then did USSR qualify at England's expense?

947.   Who finished fourth in the 1958 World Cup?

948.   Who, alongside Pelé, was the joint second top goal scorer in the 1958 World Cup finals?

949.   Who, alongside Brazil's Vavá, finished third in the 1958 World Cup scoring chart?

950.   Who scored Sweden's opening goal of the 1958 World Cup final?

CHILE 1962 REVISITED

951.   What 1960 event threatened Chile's ability to host the 1962 World Cup tournament?

952.   How many goals were scored in the 1962 World Cup finals tournament? A: 89, B: 99, C: 109, D: 119.

953.   Who scored the first goal of the 1962 World Cup finals? A: Héctor Facundo, B: Ron Flowers, C: Rolf Wüthrich, D: Mário Zagallo.

954.   Which was the first nation that England defeated in the 1962 World Cup finals?

955.   Which nation knocked West Germany out of the 1962 World Cup Quarter-finals?

956.   West Germany qualified from Group 2 alongside which South American nation?

957.   Six players shared the top goal scorer position for the 1962 World Cup finals, name the two Brazilians in that list.

958.   Which nation conceded the most goals in the group stage of the 1962 World Cup finals?

959.   Which former World Champions failed to qualify from Group 2 of the 1962 World Cup finals?

960.   Which England striker scored his only World Cup goal in his first victory of the 1962 World Cup finals?

ENGLAND 1966 REVISITED

961. Name the six venues, outside London, that hosted group games of the 1966 World Cup finals?

962. What was the name of the dog that found the stolen World Cup wrapped up in newspaper stuffed under some bushes?

963. The English FA commissioned a replica Jules Rimet trophy in case the real one was never found. Where is this copy now on display?

964. Which nation finished bottom of England's group (Group 1) in the 1966 World Cup?

965. Who scored the first goal (in relation to timing as several games kicked off at the same time) of the 1966 World Cup finals?

966. Which nation finished as runners-up in West Germany's group (Group 2) in the 1966 World Cup finals?

967. Which of the nations that won its group in the 1966 World Cup finals, scored the least goals in that phase of the tournament?

968. Which nation scored the most goals in the group stage of the 1966 World Cup finals?

969. Which nation did West Germany beat in the 1966 World Cup semi-finals?

970. Who was the top Korean goal scorer in the 1966 World Cup finals?

MEXICO 1970 REVISITED

971.   Who scored the first goal of the 1970 World Cup finals?

972.   Which two nations contested the 0-0 opening game of the 1970 World Cup finals?

973.   Which nation did Israel gain a creditable 0-0 draw against in Group 2 1970 World Cup finals?

974.   Who scored Brazil's first goal of the 1970 World Cup finals?

975.   Who scored England's only first half goal the 1970 World Cup finals?

976.   Who scored Italy's winning goal in the semi-final clash with West Germany in the 1970 World Cup finals?

977.   Name Brazil's four goal scorers in the 1970 World Cup final.

978.   Which 1966 World Cup finalist scored West Germany's last minute equaliser against Italy in the 1970 World Cup Semi-final?

979.   Which 1966 World Cup finalist scored West Germany's winner in the 1970 World Cup 3rd place play-off?

980.   Which Brazilian scored a total of 3 goals in the 1970 World Cup finals?

WEST GERMANY
1974 REVISITED

981. Who scored West Germany's first goal in the 1974 World Cup finals?

982. Which two nations played out yet another 0-0 opening game for the 1974 World Cup finals?

983. Who scored Yugoslavia's first goal in their thrashing of Zaire in Group 2 of the 1974 World Cup finals?

984. Which player scored two goals for Scotland in the 1974 World Cup finals?

985. Johan Cruyff scored two goals for Holland in their opening game against which nation in the 1974 World Cup finals?

986. East Germany scored one goal in the 1974 World Cup finals against which nation?

987. Which Dutch player shared the second top goal scorer for the 1974 World Cup finals position with Andrzej Szarmach?

988. Which Brazilian matched his goal tally for the 1970 World Cup in the 1974 World Cup finals?

989. Which nation finished third in the 1974 World Cup finals?

990. Which nation conceded 14 goals while scoring just 2 in the 1974 World Cup finals?

ARGENTINA 1978 REVISITED

991. Who scored the first goal in the 1978 World Cup finals?

992. Which nation technically knocked West Germany out of the 1978 World Cup?

993. Which player scored for both Holland and Italy in their Group A clash in the 1978 World Cup finals?

994. Scotland's Archie Gemmill scored one of the most memorable goals in the 1978 World Cup but he scored two in total. Which nation did Gemmill score his other goal against?

995. Who scored Scotland's first goal in their victory against the eventually runners-up in the 1978 World Cup finals?

996. Which nation finished fourth in the 1978 World Cup finals?

997. Which nation did joint second top scorer for the 1978 World Cup, Teófilo Cubillas play for?

998. Which player was Austria's top goal scorer for the 1978 World Cup scoring 4 goals?

999. What nation did 40-yard strike goal scorer, Arie Haan play for in the 1974 and 1978 World Cups?

1000. Who was West Germany's top goal scorer for the 1978 World Cup finals?

SPAIN 1982 REVISITED

1001. How many goals were scored in total in the 1982 World Cup finals? A: 106, B: 126, C: 136, D: 146.

1002. Who scored Argentina's first goal of the 1982 World Cup finals?

1003. Who was the referee that represented England at the 1982 World Cup finals?

1004. Who scored Italy's first goal of the 1982 World Cup finals?

1005. Which stadium staged the opening match of the 1982 World Cup finals?

1006. Who, in the 1982 World Cup finals, scored the goal that put Scotland into the lead against Brazil before they ended up losing 4-1?

1007. Who scored Scotland's fifth goal in their 1982 World Cup finals 5-2 victory against New Zealand?

1008. Who was the Polish player that shared the third place top-goal scorer position in the 1982 World Cup finals with Zico?

1009. Which Northern Ireland player finished the tournament with 3 goals in the 1982 World Cup finals?

1010. Who was the top scoring French player in the 1982 World Cup finals?

MEXICO 1986 REVISITED

1011. Which Brazilian was joint second top goal scorer alongside Diego Maradona and Emilio Butragueño in the 1986 World Cup finals?

1012. Which nation's players went on strike during the 1986 World Cup finals?

1013. Against which nation did Diego Maradona score his first goal of the 1986 World Cup finals?

1014. Which of the 1986 World Cup stadiums had the largest crowd capacity?

1015. Who scored France's first goal of the 1986 World Cup finals?

1016. Which players scored Northern Ireland's two 1986 World Cup finals goals?

1017. The Algerian who scored in the 1-1 1986 World Cup finals draw against Northern Ireland was related to a World Cup legend of the future. What was his surname?

1018. Who scored West Germany's winner against Scotland in the 1986 World Cup finals?

1019. Who scored Portugal's winner against England in the 1986 World Cup finals?

1020. Which USSR player scored a hat-trick in a Round of 16 match against Belgium but still finished on the losing team?

ITALY 1990 REVISITED

1021. When West Germany beat England in the 1990 World Cup
semi-final, which four Germans netted their penalty kicks?

1022. Who was second top goal scorer in the 1990 World Cup
finals?

1023. Who was Spain's top goal scorer in the 1990 World Cup
finals?

1024. Who was England's second top goal scorer in the 1990 World
Cup finals?

1025. Who scored Cameroon's second 1990 World Cup
quarter-final goal against England before Gary Lineker forced
the game into extra time?

1026. What nationality was the referee, José Roberto Wright for the
1990 World Cup Semi-final between West Germany and
England?

1027. In the 1990 World Cup Quarter-final between Argentina and
Yugoslavia, which Argentinean saw his spot kick saved in the
decisive penalty shootout?

1028. Who was the Republic of Ireland goalkeeper whose save
against Romania's Timofte helped his team qualify for the
1990 World Cup quarter-finals?

1029. Who was Argentina's top goal scorer in the 1990 World Cup
finals, after he scored 2 goals?

1030. How many goals were scored in total during the 1990 World
Cup finals? A: 115, B: 125, C: 135, D: 145.

USA 1994 REVISITED

1031.   Which of the 1994 World Cup finals stadium had the largest crowd capacity?

1032.   Who scored the host nation's first goal of the 1994 World Cup finals?

1033.   Who scored the goal for Brazil that knocked the host nation of the 1994 World Cup finals out of the tournament?

1034.   Which nation finished fourth in the in the 1994 World Cup finals?

1035.   Which Swedish player scored the first goal against Brazil in the 1994 World Cup finals?

1036.   Erwin Sánchez was a goal scorer for which nation in the 1994 World Cup finals?

1037.   Which nations finished third in their respective 1994 World Cup finals groups despite having won two of their matches?

1038.   How old was Cameroon's Roger Milla when he scored his last World Cup goal against Russia in the 1994 World Cup finals?

1039.   Who scored Germany's first goal of the 1994 World Cup finals?

1040.   For which nation was Ion Andoni Goikoetxea a twice goal scorer for in the 1994 World Cup finals?

FRANCE 1998 REVISITED

1041.   Against which nation did Thierry Henry score his first World Cup finals goal in the 1998 tournament?

1042.   In England's Round of 16 match against Argentina, which Argentinean had his penalty saved by David Seaman in the deciding shootout?

1043.   In the third place play-off match of the 1998 World Cup finals, who scored Holland's consolation goal?

1044.   How many goals were scored in the whole of the 1998 World Cup finals tournament? A: 161, B: 171, C: 181, D: 191.

1045.   Who scored Scotland's goal against Brazil in the 1998 World Cup finals?

1046.   What was the name of the Official mascot for the 1998 World Cup?

1047.   Which South American nation, along with Italy, qualified for the last 16 of the 1998 World Cup from Group B?

1048.   Which future English Premiership player scored South Africa's first goal in the 1998 World Cup finals?

1049.   Who scored France's first goal in the 1998 World Cup finals against South Africa?

1050.   Against which nation was Zinadine Zidane sent off in the 1998 World Cup finals?

KOREA/JAPAN 2002 REVISITED

1051.   What was the name of the three World Cup 2002 mascots?

1052.   Which nation did USA gain a surprise 3-2 victory against in Group D of the 2002 World Cup finals?

1053.   Who scored a hat-trick for Portugal against Poland in the 2002 World Cup finals?

1054.   Which Swedish player scored a sensational free kick against Argentina in Group F of the 2002 World Cup finals?

1055.   Name the Japanese player who scored two goals in the 2002 World Cup finals?

1056.   Two Spaniards scored three goals for their nation in the 2002 World Cup Raúl and who else?

1057.   Who was the referee of the 2002 World Cup final?

1058.   Which nation knocked Spain out of the 2002 World Cup finals?

1059.   Tunisia scored one goal in the 2002 World Cup finals, against which nation?

1060.   Which nation knocked Japan out of the 2002 World Cup finals in the Round of 16?

GERMANY 2006 REVISITED

1061. Who scored two goals for Costa Rica against Germany in the opening match of the 2006 World Cup finals?

1062. Who scored Poland's only two goals of the 2006 World Cup finals against Costa Rica?

1063. England's opening goal in the 2006 World Cup finals was credited as an own goal against which Paraguayan player?

1064. Who was the first England player to score in the 2006 World Cup finals?

1065. Which English Premiership player scored the Ivory Coast's first goal of the 2006 World Cup finals?

1066. Which nation did Argentina beat 6-0 in Group C of the 2006 World Cup finals?

1067. Which English Premier League player scored Holland's first goal of the 2006 World Cup finals?

1068. Which was the only nation to take a point from Italy during the group phase of the 2006 World Cup finals?

1069. Which African nation finished bottom of Group G in the 2006 World Cup finals and competed against Switzerland, France and Korean Republic?

1070. Which nation knocked Argentina out of the 2006 World Cup Quarter-finals?

ALAN BALL

1071.   What was Alan Ball's full name?

1072.   Where in England was Alan Ball born?

1073.   With which youth club did Alan Ball begin his football career?

1074.   With which club did Alan Ball make the most appearances in his career?

1075.   In what year did Alan Ball make his England debut?

1076.   In what year did Alan Ball first join Southampton?

1077.   How many England caps did Alan Ball win? A: 62, B: 72, C: 82, D: 92.

1078.   After the 1966 World Cup Final Alan Ball swapped his shirt with which player?

1079.   In what year was Alan Ball awarded the MBE?

1080.   What club did Alan Ball manage in between being sacked by Portsmouth and hired by Southampton?

WORLD CUP TRIVIA - I

1081. What number shirt did Brazil's Adriano wear at the 2006 World Cup finals?

1082. Who wore the number 17 shirt for Portugal at the 2006 World Cup finals?

1083. What number shirt did Robbie Keane wear for the Republic of Ireland at the 2002 World Cup finals?

1084. Rivaldo of Brazil pretended to be hit in the face by the ball and rolled around as if he were seriously injured when he had actually only been hit on the arm. Against which nation was he playing?

1085. Which French player was sent off in the 1998 World Cup final?

1086. What is the name of the referee who sent David Beckham off in the 1998 World Cup finals?

1087. Against which nation was Holland playing when Johan Cruyff famously executed 'The Cruyff Turn' at the 1974 World Cup?

1088. Why was Chile disallowed from participating in the 1994 World Cup qualifying competition?

1089. Against which nation did France gain their only point of the 1966 World Cup?

1090. Which team beat Scotland 7-0 in the 1954 World Cup finals?

WORLD CUP TRIVIA - 2

1091. Which legendary Scotish striker retired after the 1974 World Cup finals?

1092. Who captained Mexico's 1986 World Cup final squad?

1093. In which minute of the match did Diego Maradona score his famous 'Hand of God' goal against England in the 1986 World Cup finals? A: 51st, B: 56th, C: 61st, D: 66th.

1094. In which year did Honduras qualify for it's only World Cup finals?

1095. In which year did Cuba reach the quarter-finals of the World Cup?

1096. What was the first African nation to compete in a World Cup finals tournament?

1097. Who was the first player to score for Jamaica in a World Cup finals game?

1098. Which nation will host the 2010 World Cup finals?

1099. Why will the 2014 World Cup be a landmark for the competition?

1100. As of 2007, who what was the only nation to table a confident bid to stage the 2014 World Cup finals?

GERMANY (WEST)

1101. In what year did Germany first compete in an international football match?

1102. Which German player finished his international career on 101 caps in 2000?

1103. Who replaced Jürgen Klinsmann as Germany's head coach after the 2006 World Cup?

1104. Which one of the following statements is false? A: Germany is the only nation to have won the men and womens' World Cups? B: Germany does not have a national stadium. C: Germany's original kit was red shirts with white shorts. D: Adidas has provided the German football kit since 1954.

1105. Germany is the only nation to have had its goalkeeper win the Player of the Tournament award at a World Cup. Name the player that achieved this.

1106. What was the last World Cup in which 'West' Germany featured?

1107. As of 2007, how many World and European championships had Germany won?

1108. What was the first World Cup finals to feature Germany?

1109. How many times have Germany reached at least the last four of the World Cup?

1110. As of 2007 who was the last nation to beat Germany in a penalty shootout in Euro 76?

TRIVIA ASSORTMENT

1111. How many European countries took part in the 1998 World Cup finals?

1112. In 1996 a World Cup qualifier between Scotland and Estonia was abandoned, why?

1113. What nickname does the Australian national team have?

1114. Only two Manchester United players appeared in the 1994 World Cup, name them.

1115. How many players who have played for or would go on to play for Arsenal took part in the 1998 World Cup final?

1116. Which legendary coach led West Germany to first second and third place in the World Cup and first and second in the European Championships?

1117. Mustapha El Hadji emerged as one of the stars of the 1998 World Cup finals, which nation did he play for?

1118. Who took over has manager of the German national team after Franz Beckenbauer?

1119. What was the first nation to win the World Cup after failing to qualify for the previous tournament?

1120. In 1994 the US World Cup committee stated that 'three countries in the world that would have caused us logistical and security problems, so we are very pleased they're not coming.' Those nations were Iran, Iraq and who else?

ARGENTINA

1121. By what nickname is the Argentinean national team known in Argentina?

1122. Argentina played its first international in 1901 against which nation?

1123. Argentina achieved their biggest win (12-0) on January 22nd 1942 against which nation?

1124. Which nation inflicted one of Argentina's biggest defeats (6-1) on June 15th 1958?

1125. How many times has Argentina reached the last four of the World Cup?

1126. As of 2007, only three players had won more than 100 caps for Argentina, name one of them.

1127. Gabriel Batistuta is Argentina's all-time top goal scorer, but who is second?

1128. Which nation has Argentina played the most times in its history (record in international football)?

1129. What is the name of the stadium in which Argentina play their home games?

1130. Who became Argentina's head coach in 2006?

YET ANOTHER ROUND OF TRIVIA

1131.   In 1974 World Cup the first penalty in a final was awarded for a foul against which player?

1132.   Belgium international, Luis Oliveira was born in what country?

1133.   Brazil's Ronaldo was playing for which club at the time of the 1998 World Cup finals?

1134.   What was the first World Cup to benefit from satellite technology and therefore be seen on a global scale?

1135.   Who took over from Bryan Hamilton as manager of Northern Ireland after they had failed to qualify for the 1998 World Cup finals?

1136.   Who scored Italy's goal when they became the first nation to beat England in a World Cup qualifier at Wembley Stadium in 1997?

1137.   In which World Cup final was a goal scored without the conceding nation having touched the ball?

1138.   Jan Cuelemans was a World Cup player for which nation?

1139.   What club did Gary Lineker join after the 1986 World Cup finals?

1140.   In each of the two years prior to the 1966 World Cup final, Bobby Moore had won a major trophy with West Ham at Wembley, which ones?

URUGUAY

1141. As of 2007, who is the Uruguayan player who has won the most caps for his country?

1142. What colour are the shirts of the Uruguayan second kit?

1143. Who is the Uruguayan all time top goal scorer (as of 2007)?

1144. Who became Uruguay's head coach in 2006?

1145. In what year did Uruguay last reach the World Cup semi-finals?

1146. Since 1974, how many times has Uruguay failed to qualify for the World Cup finals?

1147. In what year did Uruguay last win the Copa America?

1148. Name the Uruguayan international who played for Manchester United between 2002 and 2004.

1149. What is the name of Uruguay's home stadium?

1150. What three letters appear on the Uruguayan team logo?

TER-IVIA

1151. How many World Cup finals tournaments did Northern Ireland compete in under Billy Bingham?

1152. Three West Ham United players played in the 1966 World Cup final name them.

1153. Which player scored for Scotland in the 1974, 1978 and 1982 World Cup finals?

1154. How many matches did Jimmy Greaves play in during the 1966 World Cup finals?

1155. When did Scotland last win a match in the finals of a World Cup?

1156. Who is the last player to win the World Cup Golden Boot by scoring more than six goals?

1157. Name the German player who was sent home from the 1994 World Cup after making gestures to a crowd?

1158. Scotland has played 23 games in World Cup finals, how many of them did they win?

1159. Why was Redondo left out of the 1998 Argentinean World Cup squad?

1160. Against which nation did Northern Ireland legend Pat Jennings win his last international cap in the 1986 World Cup finals?

FRANCE

1161. How many times has France reached at least the last four of the World Cup?

1162. As of 2007, who is France's most capped player?

1163. Who is France's all time top goal scorer?

1164. Against which nation did France play its first international match in May 1904?

1165. Which nation inflicted France's biggest defeat (17-1) in 1908?

1166. France achieved their biggest victory in 1995 (10-0) against which country?

1167. How many times has France failed to qualify for the World Cup finals?

1168. Who was the coach who steered France to World Cup glory in 1998?

1169. Who took over as French national coach in 1998 and was in charge when France won the 2000 European Championships?

1170. Against which nation did France achieve their first win in World Cup finals?

A FURTHER ROUND
OF TRIVIA

1171. Who was head coach of France during the 2006 World Cup?

1172. What three letters appear in the French logo that appears on players' shirts?

1173. How many times has USA reached the last four of a World Cup finals tournament?

1174. How many times has Sweden reached the last four of a World Cup finals tournament?

1175. Name the three nations that have finished runners-up twice but have never won the World Cup.

1176. How many times has Spain reached the last four of the World Cup?

1177. Before winning the World Cup in 1978, how many times had Argentina reached the last four in the tournament?

1178. Which is the only nation outside Europe/USSR and America to reach the last four of the World Cup?

1179. What was the first World Cup final to go to extra-time?

1180. Poland have finished in the last four of the World Cup twice, in 1974 and when else?

ENGLAND - I

1181.   Steve McClaren's assistant's were Terry Venables and who else?

1182.   Name the ground where England played its first international match in 1872.

1183.   In what year did England first wear numbered shirts?

1184.   How many times has England failed to qualify for the World Cup finals since 1970?

1185.   As of the end of the 2008 World Cup name the five players to have made over 100 appearances for England.

1186.   Stanley Matthews England career covered how many years?

1187.   Who became England's youngest player on May 30th 2006?

1188.   The record of the shortest England international career is just six minutes in 1980. Who is the player with that distinction?

1189.   Which player made the most England appearances without ever appearing in a World Cup finals tournament?

1190.   How many World Cup finals did Stanley Matthews feature in?

ENGLAND - 2

1191.   Who was the last England player to make his international debut at a World Cup finals tournament?

1192.   Who is the youngest player to feature for England in a World Cup finals tournament?

1193.   Which two players share the record for most appearances for England in World Cup finals having both played 20 matches each?

1194.   Which England player has made the most appearances for England without playing in either the World Cup finals or the European Championship finals?

1195.   Which England player has appeared in the most consecutive finals tournaments of the World Cup and European Championships between 1996 and 2006?

1196.   Which player has made the most appearances for England while not playing for an English club?

1197.   Which club's players has won the most England caps in total (over 960 as of September 2007)?

1198.   Michael Owen scored his 40th England goal in a Euro 2008 Qualifier against which nation at Wembley Stadium in September 12th 2007?

1199.   Who scored the first goal in and England shirt at the new Wembley Stadium for England U21s in March 2007 against Italy U21s?

1200.   How many different stadiums did England play home matches in while the new Wembley Stadium was being built?

ANSWERS

ORIGINS
1.   The Goddess Of Victory.
2.   Abel Lafleur.
3.   Henri Delauney.
4.   Because the Olympic football tournament was strictly only for amateur players FIFA felt that they should create a competition for the best players in the world, be them professional or amateur.
5.   Sir Thomas Lipton.
6.   Turin.
7.   Uruguay.
8.   Italy, Holland, Hungary, Spain, Sweden and Uruguay.
9.   Montevideo.
10.   Winged Victory of Samothrace. (AKA Nike of Samothrace).

URUGUAY 1930
11.   Mexico and France.
12.   Pocitos Stadium in Montevideo.
13.   It is the only city to have staged every match of a whole World Cup Finals tournament.
14.   USA.
15.   Uruguay.
16.   Yugoslavia.
17.   Argentina.
18.   6-1.
19.   Estadio Centenario (Centenary Stadium).
20.   Pablo Dorado.

JULES RIMET
21.   1921.
22.   Theuley-les-Lavoncourt, France.
23.   He was a lawyer.
24.   Croix de Guerre.
25.   1954.
26.   14 inches.

27.	1956.
28.	Lausanne.
29.	1983.
30.	1956.

ITALY 1934

31.	Benito Mussolini.
32.	Vittorio Pozzo.
33.	Stadoi Nazionale del Partiti Nazionale Fascista. (PNF Stadium).
34.	USA (7-1).
35.	16.
36.	There was no group stage and they were knocked out in the first round.
37.	The San Siro Stadium.
38.	Egypt.
39.	Argentina.
40.	Oldrich Nejedly.

FRANCE 1938

41.	Because of the Spanish Civil War.
42.	England.
43.	15.
44.	Parc des Princes.
45.	Dutch East Indies.
46.	Brazil and Cuba.
47.	Stade Olympique de Columbes, Paris.
48.	Italy 4 Hungary 2.
49.	The Coupe du Monde.
50.	Brazil and Sweden (Brazil won 4-2).

BRAZIL 1950

51.	183,000.
52.	199,854.
53.	England 2 Chile 0.
54.	Spain.
55.	Spain.
56.	Ademir (Brazil) 7goals.
57.	13.
58.	Joseph 'Larry' Gaetjens.
59.	Friaça.
60.	Uruguay 2 Brazil 1.

SWITZERLAND 1954

61.	Germany (West).
62.	Uruguay.
63.	Puskás
64.	Uruguay.
65.	South Korea.
66.	11.
67.	Hungary 8 West Germany 3.

68. Wankdorf Stadium (in Berne).
69. Helmut Rahn.
70. Fritz Walter.

FERENC PUSKÁS
71. 1927.
72. A: 87.
73. Real Madrid.
74. Budapest.
75. Spain.
76. D: 83 (in 84 games).
77. Kispest Honved.
78. The Galloping Major.
79. 1956.
80. 1966.

SWEDEN 1958
81. Just Fontaine (13 goals).
82. 6.
83. Brazil 5 Sweden 2.
84. Soviet Union and Austria.
85. Luiz Bellini.
86. Northern Ireland (1-0 versus Czechoslovakia).
87. Brazil (1-0).
88. Stockholm.
89. Peter McParland.
90. France (6-3 versus West Germany).

RAYMOND KOPA
91. France.
92. Stade Reims
93. 1958.
94. Real Madrid.
95. He is the only player, so far (as of 2007) to have won the young player of the tournament and the senior version of the award in the World Cups of 1954 and 1958.
96. Kopaszewski.
97. Nœux-les-Mines, Pas-de-Calais.
98. Pelé.
99. 1962.
100. 3 times with Real Madrid (1957, 1958 and 1959).

JUST FONTAINE
101. His 13 goals in the 1958 World Cup is still a record in 2007.
102. Marrakesh in Morocco.
103. Nice.
104. 30.
105. France and Morocco.
106. Paris St Germaine.
107. 27.

108.   US Casablanca.
109.   Stade Reims.
110.   1933.

PELÉ (PART 1)
111.   Edson Arantes.
112.   Tres Coracoes.
113.   1973.
114.   Santos.
115.   4 (1958, 1962, 1966 and 1970).
116.   1,283.
117.   12.
118.   Wales.
119.   France.
120.   Minister of Sport for Brazil.

CHILE 1962
121.   Argentina.
122.   Czechoslovakia.
123.   Florian Albert.
124.   1 (versus Mexico).
125.   Garrincha.
126.   Garrincha.
127.   Ken Aston.
128.   The White Pelé.
129.   Chile (beat Yugoslavia in the Third-Place play-off).
130.   Yugoslavia (1-0).

GARRINCHA
131.   Manoel Francisco dos Santos.
132.   Botafogo.
133.   The Joy of the People.
134.   Elza Soares.
135.   1955 (versus Chile).
136.   50.
137.   14.
138.   1966.
139.   1972.
140.   49.

ENGLAND 1966
141.   Sir Stanley Rous.
142.   World Cup Willie.
143.   Liverpool.
144.   Uruguay.
145.   White City Stadium, London. (Uruguay v France).
146.   Eusébio.
147.   North Korea.
148.   Helmut Haller (West Germany) 5 goals.
149.   Helmut Schön.

150.   Goodison Park (Everton FC).

JACK CHARLTON
151.   20 (1953-1973).
152.   Middlesborough.
153.   Jackie Milburn.
154.   Coal mining.
155.   1970.
156.   1967.
157.   Eoin Hand.
158.   1935 (May 8th).
159.   1965.
160.   Twice (1968 and 1971).

EUSÉBIO
161.   Eusébio da Silva Ferreira
162.   Mozambique.
163.   Benfica.
164.   The Black Panther or the Black Pearl.
165.   1965.
166.   1962.
167.   1973.
168.   1 (1966).
169.   B: 41.
170.   1942.

SIR ALF RAMSAY
171.   1950.
172.   Dagenham.
173.   1999.
174.   Southampton.
175.   Tottenham Hotspur.
176.   Ipswich Town.
177.   Birmingham City.
178.   1974.
179.   Panathinaikos.
180.   Right-Back.

SIR BOBBY CHARLTON
181.   Preston North End.
182.   1937.
183.   Waterford United.
184.   106.
185.   1984.
186.   4 (1958, 1962, 1966 and 1970).
187.   West Germany (1970 World Cup).
188.   David Beckham.
189.   Suzanne.

190.	1994.

SIR GEOFF HURST
191.	Charles.
192.	1959.
193.	Essex (versus Lancashire).
194.	Stoke City.
195.	Romania.
196.	A: 49.
197.	West Bromwich Albion.
198.	Chelsea.
199.	Lancashire (Ashton-under-Lyne).
200.	Hans Tilkowski.

FRANZ BECKENBAUER
201.	1945.
202.	Hamburg SV.
203.	D: 103.
204.	1977.
205.	New York Cosmos.
206.	Olympique de Marseille.
207.	5 (1966, 1970, 1974, 1986 and 1990).
208.	Der Kaiser.
209.	5 (4 in 1966, 1 in 1970 0 in 1974).
210.	1974 -1976.

MEXICO 1970
211.	Soviet Union.
212.	Romania.
213.	Gerd Müller.
214.	England.
215.	Italy.
216.	Peru.
217.	West Germany beat Uruguay 1-0.
218.	El Salvador.
219.	Mexico.
220.	Jairzinho.

JAIRZINHO
221.	Jair Ventura Filho.
222.	Garrincha.
223.	1982.
224.	Olympique De Marseille.
225.	Zaire.
226.	1944.
227.	B: 33.
228.	Ronaldo.
229.	Argentina (1974 Semi-final group E).

230.   C: 3rd.

BOBBY MOORE
231.   Chelsea.
232.   1965.
233.   Southend United.
234.   Columbia.
235.   1958.
236.   1964.
237.   Jimmy Ruffell.
238.   C: £25,000.
239.   1977.
240.   1993 (February 24th).

CARLOS ALBERTO
241.   Azerbaijan.
242.   Carlos Alberto Torres.
243.   1944.
244.   New York Cosmos.
245.   1964.
246.   Santos FC.
247.   D: 8.
248.   1977.
249.   B: 53.
250.   1982.

PELÉ (PART 2)
251.   Bobby Moore.
252.   1940.
253.   Manchester United.
254.   D: 77.
255.   1957.
256.   Uwe Seeler. (West Germany 1958-1970)
257.   Escape to Victory.
258.   Mike Bassett: England Manager.
259.   1997.
260.   Fulham FC.

WEST GERMANY 1974
261.   Zaire.
262.   Peter Lorimer.
263.   Paul Breitner.
264.   East Germany.
265.   Haiti.
266.   Grzegorz Lato (Poland).
267.   Jack Taylor.
268.   Carlos Caszely of Chile versus West Germany.
269.   Olympic Stadium, Munich.

270.   Scotland.

JOHAN CRUYFF
271.   Hendrik Johannes Cruijff.
272.   1947.
273.   Barcelona.
274.   Los Angeles Aztecs.
275.   1964.
276.   1966.
277.   Feyenoord.
278.   4 (1971, 1972 and 1973 with Ajax as a player and 1992 with Barcelona as coach).
279.   14 times. (8 times as a player with Ajax. 1 time as a player with Feyenoord. 1 time as a player with Barcelona. 4 times as coach of Barcelona)
280.   Gerd Müller.

GERD MÜLLER
281.   Bayern Munich.
282.   D: 68.
283.   C: 403.
284.   1972 European Championship.
285.   2000.
286.   3 (1974, 1975 and 1976).
287.   Fort Lauderdale Strikers.
288.   14 (10 in 1970, 4 in 1974).
289.   1966.
290.   Der bomber.

ARGENTINA 1978
291.   Paulo Rossi (versus France).
292.   Clive Thomas.
293.   Italy.
294.   Mario Kempes (Argentina).
295.   Sweden.
296.   It was the 1000th goal in World Cup history.
297.   Willie Johnston.
298.   Tunisia (versus Mexico 3-1).
299.   The penalty shootout.
300.   Leopoldo Luque.

MARIO KEMPES
301.   1954.
302.   Valencia.
303.   César Luis Menotti.
304.   1973.
305.   3 (1974, 1978 and 1982).
306.   El Matador (The Killer).
307.   Instituto.

308. Holland (1978 World Cup Final).
309. 6 (all in 1978).
310. C: Alberto.

ARCHIE GEMMILL
311. St Mirren.
312. Preston North End.
313. 15
314. Birmingham City.
315. Jacksonville Tea Men.
316. Kenny Dalglish.
317. Scot Gemmill.
318. Derby County.
319. B: 43.
320. 1947.

OSVALDO ARDILES
321. Huracán.
322. 1973.
323. Swindon Town.
324. Paris St Germain.
325. Because of the Falklands War.
326. 1.
327. Blackburn Rovers.
328. Pitón.
329. West Bromwich Albion.
330. Racing Club de Avellaneda (in 2002-2003).

SPAIN 1982
331. Erwin Vandenburgh (Belgium).
332. John Wark.
333. Gerry Armstrong.
334. Sócrates.
335. Paolo Rossi (Italy).
336. Italy.
337. Poland (2-0).
338. Bernabéu Stadium (Real Madrid FC).
339. Paul Breitner.
340. Karl-Heinz Rummenigge.

PAOLO ROSSI
341. Vicenza.
342. 1977.
343. Michel Platini (1983).
344. Zico (Brazil).
345. AC Milan.
346. C: 20.
347. He was incorrectly found guilty of being involved in a betting scandal (Totonero)
348. 3

349.	Enzo Bearzot
350.	1986.

BRYAN ROBSON
351.	1975.
352.	Bradford City.
353.	1981.
354.	France.
355.	Hakan Sükür (Turkey versus South Korea).
356.	3 (1982, 1986 and 1990).
357.	Lennie Lawrence.
358.	£1.5 million.
359.	Captain Marvel.
360.	The European Cup Winners Cup.

GIUSEPPE BERGOMI
361.	1963.
362.	1982.
363.	Internazionale, Milan.
364.	4 (1982, 1986, 1990 and 1998).
365.	B: 81.
366.	1999.
367.	Lo Zio (The Uncle).
368.	Brazil.
369.	Alessandro Nesta.
370.	3 (1990-91, 1993-94, 1997-98).

MICHEL PLATINI
371.	Michel François Platini.
372.	St Étienne or AS Nancy-Lorraine.
373.	1976.
374.	True, he signed professional terms with Nancy after the competition.
375.	3 (1978, 1982 and 1986).
376.	Spain.
377.	2007.
378.	3 (1983, 1984 and 1985).
379.	Diego Maradona.
380.	Lennart Johansson.

DINO ZOFF
381.	1942.
382.	He is the oldest player to have won the World Cup (Spain 1982).
383.	D: 112.
384.	SS Lazio
385.	1968.
386.	Udinese.
387.	1998.
388.	Marco Ballotta (SS Lazio) and Paolo Maldini (AC Milan).
389.	1968.

390. Cesare Maldini.

MEXICO 1986
391. Columbia.
392. Pique.
393. Azteca.
394. George Courtney.
395. Gary Lineker (England) 6 goals.
396. Alessandro Altobelli.
397. Canada.
398. Morocco.
399. José Luis Brown.
400. Belgium.

DIEGO MARADONA
401. Armando.
402. 1960.
403. Boca Juniors.
404. 1977.
405. £5 million.
406. Napoli (259 appearances).
407. 4 (1982, 1986, 1990, 1994).
408. Hungary (1982). Argentina won 4-1.
409. Greece in 1994.
410. 16 games as captain of his country.

GARY LINEKER
411. Everton.
412. Winston.
413. Leicester City.
414. Geri Halliwell (second cousin).
415. 10 (6 in 1986 4 in 1990).
416. 48.
417. Nagoya Grampus Eight.
418. Underground Ernie.
419. 1989.
420. Harry Kewell.

SIR BOBBY ROBSON
421. 1933.
422. Fulham.
423. 1962.
424. Fulham, Ipswich Town and Newcastle United.
425. West Bromwich Albion.
426. 4 (1958 and 1962 as a player / 1986 and 1990 as a manager).
427. Portman Road (Ipswich Town FC).
428. 1981.
429. PSV Eindhoven, Sporting Clube De Portugal, FC Porto and Barcelona.

430.   Vancouver Royals.

JOSÉ LUIS BROWN
431.   Estadiantes.
432.   1983.
433.   Tata.
434.   I (In the 1986 final).
435.   Real Murcia.
436.   French.
437.   Racing Club Avellaneda.
438.   Nacional de Medellin.
439.   Carlos Bilardo.
440.   1956.

PETER SHILTON
441.   125.
442.   C: 32.
443.   10.
444.   Fabien Barthez (France).
445.   Wimbledon, West Ham United and Coventry.
446.   17.
447.   Leyton Orient.
448.   Southampton (1984).
449.   B: FA Cup.
450.   B: Stoke City (110). (Leicester :-286. Nottingham Forest :-202 and Derby County :-175).

ITALY 1990
451.   François Omam-Biyik (Cameroon).
452.   David O'Leary.
453.   Argentina.
454.   Salvatore Schillaci.
455.   Andreas Brehme.
456.   England.
457.   B: 2.
458.   Mark Wright.
459.   Lothar Matthäus.
460.   Roger Milla (Cameroon).

PAULO MALDINI
461.   1988.
462.   AC Milan.
463.   1994.
464.   A: 126.
465.   1989.
466.   Cesare Maldini.
467.   2002.
468.   Runner-up in 1994.
469.   23 (1984-85 - 2006-07).

470.   8 (a record shared with Francisco Gento).

JÜRGEN KLINSMANN
471.   1964.
472.   VfB Stuttgart.
473.   1987.
474.   11 (3 in 1990, 5 in 1994 and 3 in 1998).
475.   Bronze.
476.   Bayern Munich.
477.   2004.
478.   Internazionale Milan.
479.   1996.
480.   Stuttgart Kickers.

RUDI VÖLLER
481.   1960.
482.   2002.
483.   3 (1986, 1990 and 1994).
484.   Werder Bremen.
485.   AS Roma.
486.   Olympique Marseille.
487.   Bayer Leverkusen.
488.   Frank Rijkaard.
489.   1860 Munich.
490.   1994.

TOTÒ SCHILLACI
491.   Salvatore Schillaci.
492.   Juventus.
493.   6.
494.   Messina.
495.   1964.
496.   Azeglio Vicini.
497.   Austria.
498.   England (Third place play-off).
499.   A: 16.
500.   Japan.

PAUL GASCOIGNE
501.   Gateshead.
502.   Jack Charlton.
503.   Denmark.
504.   Everton.
505.   Thomas Berthold.
506.   Rangers (1996 and 1997).
507.   1990.
508.   One (1990).
509.   Gary Charles.
510.   Burnley.

USA 1994

511.   Hristo Stoichkov (Bulgaria). Oleg Salenko (Russia).

512.   Jürgen Klinsmann, Germany versus Bolivia.

513.   Andrés Escobar.

514.   Philip Don.

515.   Oleg Salenko.

516.   Greece.

517.   Ray Houghton.

518.   It was the first ever World Cup match to be played indoors.

519.   Sweden.

520.   Roberto Baggio.

DUNGA

521.   Carlos Caetano Bledorn Verri.

522.   Pisa.

523.   Silver.

524.   3 (1990, 1994 and 1998).

525.   1982.

526.   2006.

527.   Fiorentina. (147 games).

528.   Japan.

529.   Queens Park Rangers.

530.   Dopey.

ROMÁRIO

531.   Romário de Souza Faria.

532.   1966.

533.   Vasco da Gama.

534.   PSV Eindhoven.

535.   1987.

536.   1988.

537.   1 (1994).

538.   2005.

539.   Vasco da Gama.

540.   Ronaldo.

ROBERTO BAGGIO

541.   1967.

542.   Vicenza.

543.   1988.

544.   3 (1990, 1994 and 1998).

545.   1993.

546.   Eddy Baggio.

547.   Diadora.

548.   Buddhism.

549.   Juventus.

550.   Brescia.

FRANCE 1998

551. César Sampaio (Brazil versus Scotland).
552. Stade de France (80,000).
553. Gabriel Batistuta.
554. Davor Šuker (Yugoslavia/Croatia) 6 goals.
555. Paul Durkin.
556. Brian McBride.
557. Lilian Thuram.
558. Christian Vieri.
559. Thierry Henry.
560. England.

ZINEDINE ZIDANE

561. Marseille, France
562. Cannes.
563. Bordeaux.
564. 1994.
565. Algeria.
566. Marco Materazzi.
567. 3 (1998, 2000 and 2003).
568. D: 108.
569. Real Madrid.
570. Twice with Real Madrid.

DAVID BECKHAM (PART 1)

571. Robert Joseph.
572. 1997.
573. 1999.
574. 2001.
575. Moldova.
576. 2000.
577. Deportivo de La Coruña.
578. Kirsty Howard.
579. 7.
580. Alan Shearer.

MICHAEL OWEN

581. 2001.
582. 1997.
583. Sweden.
584. Chile.
585. Romania.
586. 1998.
587. 1997-98 and 1998-99.
588. 2001.
589. Estonia.
590. Chester.

RONALDO
591. Ronaldo Luis Nazário de Lima.
592. PSV Eindhoven.
593. 1994.
594. Ronaldinho. (Little Ronaldo).
595. Morocco.
596. Internazionale Milano (Inter Milan).
597. Ghana.
598. AC Milan.
599. Emerson Fittipaldi.
600. 8.

HENRIK LARSSON
601. Feyenoord.
602. Helsingborg.
603. 1993.
604. Bulgaria.
605. 5 (1 in 1994, 3 in 2002 and 1 in 2006).
606. Germany (Sweden lost 2-0 in 2006 World Cup finals round of 16).
607. 4 (1997-98, 2000-01, 2001-02 and 2003-04).
608. MBE.
609. C: UEFA Cup.
610. 2 (2004-05 and 2005-06 with Barcelona).

RONALDINHO
611. Paris Saint-Germain.
612. 1999.
613. Ronaldo de Assís Moreira.
614. Rivaldo and Ronaldo.
615. Danny Mills.
616. 2 (2 in 2002 and 0 in 2006).
617. Twice (2004 and 2005).
618. 2006 (with Barcelona).
619. 1980.
620. Grêmio.

MIROSLAV KLOSE
621. Poland.
622. Kaiserslautern.
623. 10. (5 in each).
624. Saudi Arabia.
625. Werder Bremen.
626. 2006.
627. Bayern Munich.
628. Argentina (Quarter-final).
629. They were all headers.
630. A front-flip.

DAVID SEAMAN

631. Peterborough United.
632. 1990.
633. Tournoi de France.
634. 3 (1991, 1998 and 2002).
635. 200 (Seaman 75, Shilton 125).
636. 4 (1993, 1998, 2002 and 2003).
637. Tunisia in 1998.
638. C: 405.
639. 1997.
640. 1988.

FABIEN BARTHEZ

641. Allain.
642. Toulouse.
643. 1994.
644. AS Monaco.
645. Laurent Blanc.
646. Olympique de Marseille.
647. 2 (2001 and 2003).
648. He is the first goalkeeper to prevent Brazil from scoring in two
      consecutive meetings in World Cup finals tournaments. (1998 and 2006).
649. Nantes.
650. 2 (versus Denmark and Croatia).

MICHAEL BALLACK

651. 1976.
652. Chemnitzer.
653. 1999.
654. Kaiserslautern.
655. Scotland.
656. Nothing, he was a Bosman Free.
657. Saudi Arabia.
658. None.
659. 13.
660. Werder Bremen.

DENNIS BERGKAMP

661. Ajax Amsterdam.
662. Denis Law.
663. 1995.
664. 1990.
665. Morocco.
666. Argentina.
667. 2000. (After the Euro 2000 tournament).
668. 1998.
669. He had a fear of flying.
670. The Non-flying Dutchman.

KOREA/JAPAN 2002
671. Graham Poll.
672. Papa Bouba Diop (Senegal versus France).
673. France.
674. Rivaldo (Brazil).
675. South Korea.
676. Robbie Keane.
677. Turkey.
678. South Korea.
679. Mexico.
680. Michael Owen (versus Brazil).

RIVALDO
681. Vítor Borba Ferreira.
682. Deportivo de La Coruña.
683. Barcelona.
684. 2003.
685. Morocco.
686. 8 (3 in 1998, 5 in 2002).
687. Olympiakos.
688. AC Milan.
689. AEK Athens.
690. 1999.

ROBERTO CARLOS
691. Roberto Carlos da Silva.
692. Fenerbahçe.
693. China.
694. 1998.
695. 3 (1997-98, 1999-00, 2001-02).
696. Internazionale (Inter Milan).
697. France.
698. 4 (1996-97, 2000-01, 2002-03, 2006-07).
699. 1996.
700. None. (Real Madrid won the trophy in 1993, 3 years before Roberto
Carlos joined them).

ALESSANDRO DEL PIERO
701. 1974.
702. Calcio Padova
703. 1995.
704. Mexico (2002).
705. Torchbearer.
706. It was the latest goal ever scored in a World Cup finals match, (120
minutes).
707. 1997 and 1998.
708. He is the club's all-time top goal scorer.
709. 1996.
710. Sampdoria.

RAÚL
711. Raúl González Blanco.
712. Real Madrid.
713. 1994.
714. He became the first player to score 50 goals in the Champions League.
715. Nigeria.
716. 5 (1 in 1998, 3 in 2002 and 1 in 2006).
717. Spanish national team's all time top goal scorer.
718. Jorge Valdano.
719. 7.
720. 2002.

LUÍS FIGO
721. 1972.
722. Lisbon.
723. Sporting CP.
724. Barcelona.
725. 1991.
726. None.
727. A: 127.
728. 7.
729. 2001.
730. Internazionale.

DAVID BECKHAM
731. Fabio Cappello.
732. Because he has epilepsy and the flash photography might send him into a fit.
733. He is the first Englishman to score in three different World Cup finals tournaments. (One in each of 1998, 2002 and 2006).
734. Obsessive Compulsive Disorder.
735. Brylcream.
736. 2003.
737. The Daily Mirror.
738. 2000 and 2001.
739. 2003.
740. 4.

GERMANY 2006
741. Phillip Lahm (Germany).
742. Francesco Totti.
743. Ghana.
744. Portugal (1-0 in Round of 16).
745. Owen Hargreaves.
746. Thierry Henry (France).
747. Alessandro Del Piero.
748. Zinedine Zidane.
749. David Trézéguet.
750. Josip Šimunić (Croatia).

THIERRY HENRY
751.   AS Monaco.
752.   1997.
753.   £10.5 million.
754.   Arsène Wenger.
755.   Nicolas Anelka.
756.   4 (2001-02, 2003-04, 2004-05 and 2005-06).
757.   Daniel.
758.   Aimé Jacquet.
759.   £16.1 million.
760.   Nicole Merry.

TRIVIA
761.   Pelé. (12 goals).
762.   Geoff Hurst (5 goals second to Gary Linker who scored 10).
763.   Lothar Matthäus.
764.   Vittorio Pozzo (Italy 1934 and 1938).
765.   A: He forgot to check his watch.
766.   D: He was sent off.
767.   All the flag posts went missing.
768.   Gianluca Pagliuca.
769.   He is the first player ever to score a goal in the World Cup finals (1930).
770.   Rene and Willy Van der Kerkhof of Holland.

OLIVER KAHN
771.   Karlsruher SC.
772.   1995.
773.   Andreas Köpke.
774.   Jens Lehmann.
775.   The Golden Ball for best individual performance.
776.   7. (1997, 1999, 2000, 2001, 2003, 2005 and 2006).
777.   2001.
778.   European Championships 1996.
779.   Nummer eins ("Number One").
780.   A: 86.

MARTIN PETERS
781.   1943.
782.   1966.
783.   West Ham United (302 games).
784.   1962.
785.   Norwich City.
786.   Yugoslavia.
787.   Jimmy Greaves.
788.   3rd.
789.   Sheffield United.
790.   West Germany.

MORE TRIVIA
791. Canberra, Australia.
792. He has the longest name of any player from a World Cup finals tournament.
793. Roger Milla (Cameroon) he was 42 years and 39 days old when he played against Russia in the 1994 World Cup.
794. Norman Whiteside (Northern Ireland) He was 17 years and 42 days old when he played against Yugoslavia in the 1982 World Cup finals.
795. Paulo Maldini (23 matches 1990 - 2002).
796. Cafu of Brazil (1994, 1998 and 2002).
797. Diego Maradona (Argentina) 16 matches.
798. Vavá of Brazil. (2 in 1958 and 1 in 1962).
799. Gabriel Batistuta (Argentina 1994 and in 1998).
800. Laurent Blanc (France) 1998 versus Paraguay.

LOTHAR MATTHÄUS
801. Borussia Mönchengladbach.
802. 150.
803. Internazionale. (Inter Milan).
804. 1980.
805. 1990.
806. Hungary.
807. Morocco (1986).
808. 1991.
809. Portugal.
810. Rapid Vienna (2001-2002).

GABRIEL BATISTUTA
811. Fiorentina.
812. 1991.
813. Nowhere he stayed with Fiorentina and helped them gain promotion
back to Serie A two years later.
814. Greece in 1994 (he went on to score a hat-trick).
815. 10 (4 in 1994, 5 in 1998 and 1 in 2002).
816. Daniel Passarella.
817. Claudio Ranieri.
818. C: 56.
819. Al Arabi. (A Quatari football club).
820. Sweden (World Cup 2002).

ZICO
821. Udinese.
822. Flamengo.
823. Japan.
824. 1976.
825. Peru.
826. 5 (1 in 1978, 4 in 1982, 0 in 1986).
827. Beach Soccer.
828. 1989.

829.   B: 88 games 66 goals.
830.   Argentina in 1982.

BRAZIL TRIVIA
831.   1965.
832.   Garforth Town.
833.   Exeter City.
834.   Uruguay.
835.   Preguinho.
836.   1958, 1962, 1970, 1994 and 2002.
837.   Pelé, Zico and Ronaldo.
838.   Nicaragua.
839.   18.
840.   8 (1919, 1922, 1949, 1989, 1997, 1999, 2004 and 2007).

CAFU
841.   Marcos Evangelista de Moraes.
842.   Real Zaragoza
843.   He was Brazil's most capped player.
844.   AC Milan.
845.   AS Roma.
846.   1990.
847.   Italian and Spanish.
848.   14.
849.   São Paulo.
850.   1970.

ALAN SHEARER
851.   Goalkeeper.
852.   He became the youngest player to score a hat trick in the top flight of
        English Football. Jimmy Greaves previously held the record. Shearer was
17   years and 240 days old.
853.   France. (England won 2-0).
854.   Chris Sutton.
855.   Tunisia.
856.   2 (He only played in the 1998 World Cup finals).
857.   Romania (Euro 2000).
858.   Luxembourg.
859.   260.
860.   1995.

TRIVIA RETURNS
861.   Viv Richards (Antigua and West Indies respectively).
862.   1950. (The Maracana Stadium).
863.   A dog ran on to the pitch but Greaves caught it and the match
        continued.
864.   1954.
865.   Zaire (1974).
866.   The Kuwaiti players had heard a whistle and had stopped playing.

867.   Patrick Battiston.
868.   A: He spat at him.
869.   Zeze and Aimore Moreira. (1954 and 1962 World Cups respectively).
870.   Drawn game (1-1).

PATRICK VIEIRA
871.   AS Cannes.
872.   Senegal.
873.   Arsenal.
874.   7 (Premiership 1998, 2002 and 2004 - FA Cup 1998, 2002, 2003 and 2005).
875.   Holland.
876.   2 (Both in 2006).
877.   2005
878.   14.
879.   AC Milan.
880.   Juventus were relegated in 2006 after winning Serie A and then, after being found guilty of match fixing, Juventus were relegated to Serie B. Vieira moved to Internazionale and Juventus won Serie B and Vieira won Serie A with Inter.

ITALY
881.   1910 a 6-2 win versus France.
882.   Hungary.
883.   B: Angelo Schiavio.
884.   Azzurri.
885.   1958.
886.   Luigi Riva.
887.   Juventus.
888.   Silvio Piola.
889.   1938.
890.   North Korea.

URUGUAY 1930 REVISITED
891.   France and USA.
892.   C:70.
893.   Football had been dropped from the 1928 Olympic Games.
894.   USA.
895.   C: The referee blew for time six minutes early only to be persuaded later to play on? (After protests from the French players).
896.   The teams started the match wearing the same colours.
897.   He was the first player ever to be sent off in the World Cup.
898.   Argentina.
899.   D: Guillermo Stábile.
900.   Bolivia.

ITALY 1934 REVISETED
901.   Uruguay refused to participate in protest of the lack of European representation at the World Cup of 1930.

902.	A: Oldřich Nejedlý.
903.	C: 70.
904.	Benito Mussolini.
905.	D: Ernesto Belis.
906.	Spain.
907.	Italy and Spain.
908.	Italy, Austria, Czechoslovakia and Germany.
909.	Germany.
910.	B: Angelo Schiavio.

FRANCE 1938 REVISITED

911.	C: Leônidas.
912.	Switzerland.
913.	Indonesia.
914.	B: Josef Gauchel.
915.	Brazil.
916.	Gustav Wetterström.
917.	C: France.
918.	A: He scored four goals.
919.	C: Private Investigator.
920.	C: Gyula Zsengellér.

BRAZIL 1950 REVISITED

921.	B: Admir.
922.	B: They would not be allowed to play barefoot.
923.	C: 88.
924.	C: Ademir.
925.	Bolivia. (They had lost 8-0 to Uruguay).
926.	Uruguay would still have won the World Cup as they were top of the group before the game.
927.	Sweden.
928.	A: Estanislao Basora.
929.	Scotland and Turkey.
930.	Sweden.

SWITZERLAND 1954 REVISITED

931.	C: Sándor Kocsis.
932.	D: Baltazar.
933.	Austria.
934.	Bern.
935.	Uruguay.
936.	Austria or Switzerland. (Austria won)
937.	Nat Lofthouse (3 goals).
938.	Yugoslavia.
939.	Tom Finney.
940.	Austria.

SWEDEN 1958 REVISITED

| 941. | C: Agne Simonsson. |

942. D: Mazola.
943. Just Fontaine (France)
944. Uwe Seeler.
945. B: Terry Medwin.
946. USSR had won one of their three games where as England had drawn theirs.
947. West Germany.
948. Helmut Rahn.
949. Peter McParland (Northern Ireland).
950. Nils Liedholm.

CHILE 1962 REVISITED
951. A massive earthquake (measuring 9.5 magnitude. It was the largest quake of the 20th century).
952. A: 89.
953. A: Héctor Facundo.
954. Argentina.
955. Yugoslavia.
956. Chile.
957. Garrincha and Vavá.
958. Columbia (11 goals).
959. Italy.
960. Jimmy Greaves.

ENGLAND 1966 REVISITED
961. Villa Park, Goodison Park, Old Trafford, Ayresome Park, Hillsborough, Roker Park.
962. Pickles.
963. English National Football Museum.
964. France.
965. Pelé. (Brazil v Bulgaria 12 July 1966 after 15 minutes. West Germany's Sigfried Held scored after 16 minutes in his nation's opening match against Switzerland)
966. Argentina.
967. England.
968. Portugal.
969. USSR.
970. Pak Seung-Zin. (2 Goals).

MEXICO 1970 REVISITED
971. Ildo Maneiro (Uruguay).
972. Mexico and USSR.
973. Sweden.
974. Rivelino.
975. Alan Mullery v West Germany.
976. Gianni Rivera.
977. Pelé, Gérson, Jairzinho, Carlos Alberto.
978. Karl-Heinz Schnellinger.
979. Wolfgang Overath.

980.   Rivelino.

WEST GERMANY 1974 REVISITED
981.   Paul Breitner.
982.   Brazil and Yugoslavia.
983.   Dušan Bajevi?.
984.   Joe Jordan.
985.   Argentina.
986.   Argentina.
987.   Johan Neeskens.
988.   Rivelino. (3 goals again).
989.   Poland.
990.   Haiti.

ARGENTINA 1978 REVISITED
991.   Bernard Lacombe.
992.   Austria (finished bottom of group A but beat West Germany 3-2).
993.   Ernie Brandts.
994.   Holland (He also scored a penalty in the same match).
995.   Kenny Dalglish.
996.   Italy.
997.   Peru.
998.   Hans Krankl.
999.   Holland.
1000.   Karl-Heinz Rummenigge.

SPAIN 1982 REVISITED
1001.   D: 146.
1002.   Daniel Bertoni.
1003.   Clive White.
1004.   Bruno Conti.
1005.   Camp Nou, Barcelona.
1006.   David Narey.
1007.   Steve Archibald.
1008.   Zbigniew Boniek.
1009.   Gerry Armstrong.
1010.   Alain Giresse (3 goals).

MEXICO 1986 REVISITED
1011.   Careca
1012.   Portugal.
1013.   Italy (1-1 draw).
1014.   The Azteca Sadium.
1015.   Jean-Pierre Papin.
1016.   Norman Whiteside and Colin Clarke.
1017.   Zidane (Djamel).
1018.   Klaus Allofs.
1019.   Carlos Manuel.
1020.   Igor Belanov.

ITALY 1990 REVISITED

1021. Andreas Brehme, Lothar Matthäus, Karl-Heinz Riedle, Olaf Thon.
1022. Tomas Skuhravy (Czechoslovakia).
1023. Míchel (4 goals).
1024. David Platt.
1025. Eugène Ekéké.
1026. Brazilian.
1027. Diego Maradona.
1028. Packie Bonner.
1029. Claudio Caniggia.
1030. A: 115.

USA 1994 REVISITED

1031. Rose Bowl, Los Angeles in Pasadena California. (91,000).
1032. Eric Wynalda.
1033. Bebeto.
1034. Bulgaria.
1035. Kennet Andersson.
1036. Bolivia (versus Spain).
1037. Argentina and Belgium.
1038. 42 years.
1039. Jürgen Klinsmann.
1040. Spain.

FRANCE 1998 REVISITED

1041. South Africa.
1042. Hernán Crespo.
1043. Boudewijn Zenden.
1044. B: 171.
1045. John Collins (pen).
1046. Footix.
1047. Chile.
1048. Benni McCarthy.
1049. Christophe Dugarry.
1050. Saudi Arabia.

KOREA/JAPAN 2002 REVISITED

1051. Ato, Kaz and Nik.
1052. Portugal.
1053. Pauleta.
1054. Anders Svensson.
1055. Junichi Inamoto.
1056. Fernando Morientes.
1057. Piere-Luigi Collina.
1058. Korean Republic.
1059. Belgium.
1060. Turkey.

GERMANY 2006 REVISITED

1061.   Paulo Wanchope.
1062.   Bartosz Bosacki.
1063.   Carlos Gamarra.
1064.   Peter Crouch versus Trinidad and Tobago.
1065.   Didier Drogba (Chelsea).
1066.   Serbia and Montenegro.
1067.   Arjen Robben.
1068.   USA in a 1-1 draw.
1069.   Togo.
1070.   Germany.

ALAN BALL

1071.   James Alan Ball.
1072.   Farnworth.
1073.   Bolton Wanderers.
1074.   Everton. (208).
1075.   1965.
1076.   1976.
1077.   B: 72.
1078.   Nobby Stiles.
1079.   2000.
1080.   Exeter City.

TWENTY TRIVIA

1081.   9.
1082.   Cristiano Ronaldo.
1083.   10.
1084.   Turkey.
1085.   Marcel Desailly.
1086.   Kim Nielsen.
1087.   Sweden.
1088.   Their goalkeeper Roberto Rojus had faked an injury involving a firecracker to get Chile's 1989 qualifier against Brazil abandoned. He was subsequently banned for life and Chile from the 1994 World Cup.
1089.   Mexico.
1090.   Uruguay.
1091.   Denis Law.
1092.   Hugo Sanchez.
1093.   A: 51st.
1094.   1982.
1095.   1938.
1096.   Egypt.
1097.   Robbie Earle.
1098.   South Africa.
1099.   It will be the 20th staging of the tournament.
1100.   Brazil.

GERMANY (WEST)

1101.   1908.
1102.   Thomas Häßler.
1103.   Joachim Löw.
1104.   C: Germany's original kit was red shirts with white shorts.
1105.   Oliver Kahn (2002).
1106.   Italy 1990.
1107.   6 (World Cup 1954, 1974 and 1990 - Euro 1972, 1980 and 1996).
1108.   Italy 1934.
1109.   11.
1110.   Czechoslovakia.

TRIVIA ASSORTMENT

1111.   15.
1112.   The Estonians did not turn up.
1113.   The Socceroos.
1114.   Denis Irwin and Roy Keane of Republic of Ireland.
1115.   2 Emanuel Petit and Patrick Vieira.
1116.   Helmut Schön.
1117.   Morocco.
1118.   Bertie Vogts.
1119.   France (1990).
1120.   England.

ARGENTINA

1121.   Albicelestes. (Light blue and whites) or La Selección.
1122.   Uruguay.
1123.   Ecuador.
1124.   Czechoslovakia.
1125.   4 (Runners up in 1930, 1978 Champions, 1986 Champions and Runners-up in 1990).
1126.   Roberto Ayala, Javier Zanetti or Diego Simeone.
1127.   Hernán Crespo.
1128.   Uruguay.
1129.   El Monumental.
1130.   Alfio Basile.

YET ANOTHER ROUND OF TRIVIA

1131.   Johann Cruyff.
1132.   Brazil.
1133.   Internazionale, Milan.
1134.   England 1966.
1135.   Lawrie McMenemy.
1136.   Gianfranco Zola.
1137.   1974 Holland scored against West Germany.
1138.   Belgium.
1139.   Barcelona.
1140.   FA Cup in 1964. European Cup Winners Cup in 1965.

URUGUAY
1141. Rodolfo Rodriguez.
1142. Red.
1143. Héctor Scarone.
1144. Oscar Tabarez.
1145. 1970.
1146. 5 (1978, 1982, 1994, 1998 and 2006).
1147. 1995.
1148. Diego Forlán.
1149. Estadio Centenario.
1150. AUF.

TER-IVIA
1151. Two (1982 and 1986).
1152. Bobby Moore, Martin Peters and Geoff Hurst.
1153. Joe Jordan.
1154. 3.
1155. 1990 v Sweden.
1156. Grzegorz Lato of Poland in 1974.
1157. Stefan Effenberg.
1158. 4.
1159. He had refused to get his hair cut.
1160. Brazil.

FRANCE
1161. 5 (1958, 1982, 1986, 1998 and 2006).
1162. Lilian Thuram.
1163. Thierry Henry.
1164. Belgium.
1165. Denmark.
1166. Azerbaijan.
1167. 5 (1962, 1970, 1974, 1990 and 1994) They withdrew from 1950.
1168. Aimé Jacquet.
1169. Roger Lemerre.
1170. Mexico (4-1 in 1930).

A FURTHER ROUND OF TRIVIA
1171. Raymond Domenech.
1172. FFF.
1173. Once in 1930.
1174. 4 (1938, 1950, 1958 and 1994).
1175. Holland, Czechoslovakia and Hungary.
1176. Once in 1950.
1177. Once in 1930.
1178. Korean Republic (2002).
1179. 1934 Italy versus Czechoslovakia.
1180. 1982.

ENGLAND

1181. Steve Round.
1182. Hamilton Crescent, Partick, Scotland.
1183. 1922.
1184. 3 (1974, 1978 and 1994).
1185. Peter Shilton, Bobby Moore, Bobby Charlton and Billy Wright and David Beckham
1186. 22 (1934 - 1957).
1187. Theo Walcott.
1188. Peter Ward.
1189. Dave Watson (65 caps).
1190. 1 in 1954.
1191. Allan Clarke in 1970 versus Czechoslovakia.
1192. Michael Owen (18 years 183 days in June 1998).
1193. Peter Shilton and David Beckham.
1194. Emlyn Hughes (62 caps).
1195. Sol Campbell.
1196. David Beckham 36 and counting.
1197. Manchester United.
1198. Russia.
1199. David Bentley.
1200. 14 (Old Trafford, St James' Park, Anfield, Villa Park, City of Manchester Stadium, Riverside Stadium, Portman Road, Pride Park, Walkers Stadium, Stadium of Light, St Mary's Stadium, Elland Road, Upton Park and White Hart Lane).

special days for seriously ill young adults

ABOUT
WILLOW FOUNDATION

Special days aim to provide young adults living with life-threatening conditions a chance to escape the pressures of their daily routine and share quality time with family and/or friends.

Every special day is of the young person's choosing - it could involve fulfilling a lifelong dream or it could simply offer an opportunity to bring some much needed normality back into their lives.

The Foundation will endeavour to fulfil the special day request however imaginative and, if possible, exceed expectations.

To date the charity has organised and funded special days for young adults living with a wide range of serious conditions including amongst others; cancer, motor neurone disease, cystic fibrosis, organ failure, multiple sclerosis (later stages) and heart disease.

Bob & Megs Wilson founded the Willow Foundation in memory of their daughter, Anna who died of cancer aged 31.

For more information please contact:
Willow Foundation, Willow House, 18 Salisbury Square,
Hatfield, Hertfordshire, AL9 5BE
Tel: 01707 259777   Fax: 01707 259289
or email: info@willowfoundation.org.uk